Other Books By Michael J. Kiser:

4 Book Series
"A Journey Into The Spiritual Quest Of Who We Are"

Book 1
~ The Reawakening –
Book 2
~ Why Were They Called GODS…? –
Book 3
~The Knowledge That Was Once Forbidden By Some Of The Ancient Beings –
Book 4
~ The Quantum Leap Into Consciousness –

~~~

*A Journey
Into the Spiritual
Quest of Who We Are
Book 3*

THE KNOWLEDGE
That Was Once Forbidden By Some
Of The Ancient Beings

By
Michael J. Kiser

Edited by
Heidi Erikson

DragonEye Publishing

A Journey into the Spiritual Quest of Who We Are: Book 3
The Knowledge that was once forbidden by some of the Ancient Beings

Copyright 2005
By Michael J. Kiser

Cover Design 2004 By Michael J. Kiser

All rights reserved. No reproduction without the written permission from the Author and from the Publisher.

First Edition
1st Printing April 2005

ISBN 13: 978-0-9767832-3-7 (Paperback)
ISBN 13: 978-1-61500-077-7 (EPub Ebook)
ISBN 13: 978-1-61500-173-6 (PDF)

Published by Ancient Civilizations, an Imprint of DragonEye Publishing

www.DragonEyePublishers.com
email: Orders@DragonEyePublishers.com

DragonEye Publishing
753 Linden Place, Unit A
Elmira, NY 14901 USA

CONTENTS

Kiazers' Quest   1
The Gathering   2
Zoroastrian Dualism   3
From the Beings of Beings   5

CHAPTER 1
The Thought   9

CHAPTER 2
Creations   14

CHAPTER 3
Ahriman The Destroyer   56

CHAPTER 4
The Ancient of Beings   67

CHAPTER 5
Watchers   80
Dolphins of Heaven   84

CHAPTER 6
The Knowledge   89

CHAPTER 7
Removing the Acknowledgement of
Ancient Technology and Knowledge of Life   102

CHAPTER 8
Essence of our Existence   107
Removing the Veils   109
Ever going Forward   114

A Journey into the Spiritual Quest of Who We Are – Book 3-
The Knowledge that was once forbidden by some of the Ancient Beings

Kiazer's Quest

Om!

Kiazer continues on his ongoing quest, evolving by traversing a treacherous path of destiny. In this continuing journey, Kiazer strips away the veils of illusion that obscure hidden knowledge about beings engaged in such false pretense as setting themselves up to be perceived by humanity as gods and devils.

Journey along with Kiazer as he reveals secrets guarded by the gatekeepers of all religions and governments who, for centuries and at any cost, have sequestered the true knowledge of life and who we are. What will happen when these dominionists lose their grip?
Travel within the country of Eria (known today as North America) as Kiazer witnesses the reawakening of many more people to this forbidden knowledge. How will our perceptions of reality change as people realize there is more to life than what we've been told? Join Kiazer in his quest by challenging not only religious figures but also yourself. Ask the crucial and critical questions about life. Decline to be deceived.

The Gathering

As Kiazer travels around the continent of North America he stops at a community around the Pyramid Mountain located within the continental divide of the Rocky Mountains. He gathers with a group of people around a campfire on this early evening of early spring of 2004, once again, Kiazer hopes to bring forth The Knowledge for all to remember. A Knowledge that is there for all to reawaken, which is within us all that will help everyone to reawaken to who they truly are.

This is the knowledge that some beings, which came from the stars, decided to keep the inhabitants of this world from learning of who we are. Over the past thirty-six years Kiazer had been delving ever deeper into the forbidden Knowledge of the essence of our existence, as you experience the Kiazerian journal. Explore the next level of our evolution as we all move forward. Those above and those below in the unending cycles that transcend space and time.

During Kiazer's journey's around the world for the past twenty years he's been revisiting ancient and past civilizations, Kiazer illuminates the falsehoods, lies, and deceptions of the belief systems of Terra (Earth). As he discovers a past life from over 6,000 years ago, upon the continent of Tampaurban, on the eastern side of Eria and separated by the Atlantic Ocean, in present day geography, the continent of Africa / Middle East and The Far East.

Zoroastrian Dualism

Kiazer learns he is responsible for the creation of a 6,000-year-old belief system during a previous incarnation. From 4,000 through 1,000 BCE, Kiazer was known from 4,000 years BCE to 3,000 years BCE as Zartosht, and then from 3,000 years BCE through 2,000 years BCE know as Zarathustra, then from 2,000 BCE through 1,000 BCE known as Zoroaster. Zoroaster who created the original Zoroastrians Belief system that taught about the unity of good and evil existing within us all. During the year of two thousand BCE, which is when the original concept of his belief system had been changed to the way it is taught in the world of today with all of its conceptualism of the duality of good and evil. A belief system that encourages dualism by separating entities into two opposing components: good and evil. Emphasizing, in part, that evil is composed of negative beings that should be feared!

During this time period, it becomes obvious how dualistic belief systems can be used to wield power and control over diverse cultures by claiming that neighboring cultures gods are demons and therefore evil. As such a narrow belief system spreads and is imposed upon various cultures it encounters, the potential for divisiveness and destruction also seem apparent. This is only one of many belief systems, which has gotten way out of hand. It is merely one of many belief systems, which need to end. We need to bring back a more natural/spiritual way of living.

Incidentally, it's noteworthy that this belief system brought about a dispute within Zoroaster's family, which ended his life in 1,000 B.C.E. Nearly 1,000 years later, at the start of a New Age, the time period from 1,000 BCE – 500 CE. Kiazer becomes aware that several spiritual beings will be born and they will begin teaching spiritual ways of living. Given that the religions of this period became corrupted, in comparison to the older ways of believing, many people tried to lead humanity back toward a spiritual reawakening. However, many other religious figures preferred to retain control over people through fear-based belief systems and managed to convince the people that religiosity versus spirituality is the only socially acceptable way to live. Despite the fact that religions have falsified stories throughout time, it is the authors hope that this series of books will enlighten by helping you understand what is truly going on in the world within contemporary society.

■■■

*BCE/CE: (Before Current Era – Current Era: Which are acceptable replacements for what religious people refer to as, BC (Before Christ) and AD (After Death)) BC/AD.

A Journey into the Spiritual Quest of Who We Are – Book 3-
The Knowledge that was once forbidden by some of the Ancient Beings

From the Being of Beings

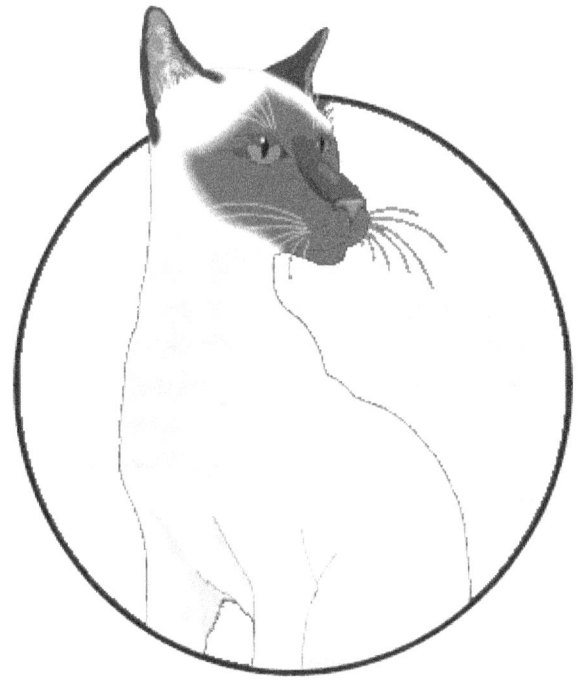

For eons…
We lived amongst you…
As many Beings…
Knowing, what you have yet to learn.

A Journey into the Spiritual Quest of Who We Are – Book 3-
The Knowledge that was once forbidden by some of the Ancient Beings

Guardians of knowledge,
That mortal minds cannot yet dream of.
For we are the keepers,
Of that is yet to come to you.

A Journey into the Spiritual Quest of Who We Are – Book 3-
The Knowledge that was once forbidden by some of the Ancient Beings

From the beings of beings.
Now, comes the time to release our
Knowledge to you…
So, you too may continue up the ladder,
Behind us, to the beyond the beyond.

A Journey into the Spiritual Quest of Who We Are – Book 3-
The Knowledge that was once forbidden by some of the Ancient Beings

Which is, rightfully yours, to take part in…
May the wings guide you,
On your journeys, to once,
Which we came from.
So, we too can continue on…
To the beyond the beyond.

Chapter 1

THE THOUGHT

As Kiazer is gathered around a campfire on this early cool evening of 2004, at the Pyramid Mountain there is a group of fifteen men and women of ages from young twenties to mid fifties. Five of these people had been traveling with Kiazer since 1993.

Kiazer mentions to the group, "five of you that have been traveling with me for a while now know about this ancient knowledge of our existence of who we are as reawakened beings, it is you will recall one aspect of thought. Well, I am going to mention the other aspect of thought. This other thought, will be, the thought that brought forth, all that there is, meaning, bringing all things into existence, including the one that many people go about calling, The One Being - GOD!

Jacobson is one of the ten people that are sitting around the campfire that are not part of the five that have been traveling with Kiazer. Jacobson is an older man in his late forties with long jet-black hair and Caucasian. He asks, "So, what you are saying is...."

Kiazer interrupts Jacobson, "Wait a minute Jacobson. I have to explain it from the beginning, or you and others will not be able to completely understand what I have to convey. There are key things that need to be made clear to everyone. Save this and all questions for the end, if you do not find the answers, by the time I am through."

Kiazer makes himself comfortable on the ground, as the evening grows darker and the campfire begins to light up the area around them. As Kiazer begins he glances around the group, "This thought, brought all things into being. It includes positive along with negative beings of all forms that are seen and unseen, matter and antimatter into physical form in one form or another.

As I mentioned to other people that I encounter through this journey of teaching to people of the knowledge that has been suppressed, thought, can be used to control and to destroy, it can be used as well to create at the same time. While one being's thought, creates life, so can another being's thought be used as a mechanism to control another being's life.

How did this come about? Well, some say in the beginning. Well, there is never a beginning. It just appears to be a beginning from that particular perspective, a viewpoint of one's own life on where they were brought into existence. This is a never-ending circle of life. As all beings come to realize, at one point or another, all beings that exist are realizing their own thoughts, are created in front of them, as well as the so called first being's thought which is also becoming created. During this time, this cycle of life we are going from, its destruction than back into being created again. Who is to say, there is only one being that can create upon the mere thought of creating and/or destroying. These are everyone's accumulated thoughts, the thoughts that create ones own existence. The thought that creates another ones thought into existence. Which also, brings forth the creation of the beings, to go with the thoughts.

This instance brings forth the beginning moments of these beings, that will exist for the experience of that thought for this creation, that they all took part in, bringing these thoughts, and all those beings of positive, negative into reality, of what may seem to be past, present and of the future. All these beings react to other beings thoughts, and they help create the world(s) around them. Based on all the thoughts that are being put out around them, some of these beings will come to see these beings as of good (positive) and evil (negative). In addition, those so-called beings of good and evil are in a way, stuck in playing this so called creation, based upon, the other beings that brought this thought into creation.

So, you have the beings that created the thought in the past, which, is now, being experienced, by the very being that created the thought without knowing, it was their own thoughts of the past. Which is now, becoming reality for them to experience their own creation that is their own worst nightmare. Because they are not aware they are their own thoughts that they are experiencing, in the present. All of the, good (creation) and evil (destruction) that these beings feared and thought of in the past, is now manifesting as their experiences. These beings had gone about creating a god, thought, and a being for all the beginning (creations) of good. They also created a being of evil, end of all things, (destruction). Some of these beings are the people of today. Twenty-five percent are realizing that they created all of these experiences they are going through, while the other seventy-five percent of the civilization are still going about thinking, that some other beings, if it be a god or some devil which created these experiences, that we are going through.

These seventy-five percent of the Earth's inhabitants are now creating a new thought of the end, of what may play out, with these two beings of light and dark. They fear what these two beings represent and fear these beings and experiences as if they were good or bad. Essentially, this is fear manifest, when people fear the experiences of what they witnessed of the past.

These people have more to fear than those two beings that were created by their own thoughts. They have the fear of the thoughts of all beings that exist.

Thoughts of positive and negative energies have always been in existence from age to age. It is the more current age that all beings fear because, they created these so called beings to represent the thoughts of positive and negative aspects of all their thought. Therefore, you have many beings that are representing good (positive) and evil (negative). All this was brought on around 7,000 BCE mainly because the people did not want to be held accountable for their thoughts and actions.

Therefore, we are living in a time, that we all must understand the thoughts that brought these so called beings into existence. Such thoughts represent the duality within all of us.

One thought ushers in the creation of life, (which you're the creator of life, the one that thought it). Which all people will witness, as being created by some being(s) therefore, the ones that end up witnessing these events are saying, "that a being of wonderful powers, brought these events, creations, into manifestation, or foretold of what will come to be." This is called, a self-fulfilling prophecy. Without realizing it was ourselves in the past that thought of the events of the future, that all of us would come to experience in time. All of us, created all of these gods and devils in the past. Most of you will come to fear your own creations as we move nearer the future. Which of these events are to come about?

We all take part in, creating all the faces of good and evil, light and dark, gods and devils, which are no more than positive and negative aspects of one's own self.

Chapter 2

THE CREATIONS

Hours passed by as everyone still sits around the campfire intrigued with all that Kiazer is sharing with him or her. "In my digging ever deeper into the mythologies, I came across a very interesting story. I am, going to share that story with you. However, this story is from a larger story, it is the fourth part of a fifteen-part book. I have the entire fifteen volumes of this story. It is a story dating from 4,000-1,000 BCE. During this time it was the age of Aries, a time of peace, harmony and tranquility.

At this time, the age that we are leaving was known as the age of Pisces. One can assume this might be where you, the civilization of now, came up with the theory of the so-called beings, of good and evil. You go about assuming that these beings will play out their roles on the Earth, of the past, present, and of the future. These Beings of dark, (evil, negativity) of now, were not on the Earth until 33,000 BCE, years ago during the beginning of this fifth cycle and the start of the age of dark and light, which is still a part of the cycle that we are experiencing. This age of dark and light is the last part of the fifth cycle of the Earth. This fifth cycle ended at the year 2000, the time the Earth's sixth cycle began.

Yes, there were other cycles and ages than the one that all of you are so used to. The past ages also had their so-called good and evil as you have learned in Book 1.

Nevertheless, the beings of good and evil of those many ages past are about to take a different turn -- a different role, so to say, for all beings of this past current cycle and age, that you are now leaving. Then you will enter into your new age of total light and total consciousness reawakening - a new way of living and understanding.

During the year of 1000 BCE this being named Ahriman was depicted as a being of evil that will come to the Earth every 1,000 years to battle the Being of Light.

During the beginning of the year 2003 I started delving into the Zoroastrian belief system. I came to learn that I was Zoroaster in my second life incarnation here on Earth. This discovery gave me another piece of the puzzle, to the bigger picture of my life, along with my personal beliefs and how the religions came about being the way they are today.

Book 4 of The Denkard of The Zoroastrian religion, which was written around 4000 BCE, or 6,000 years ago, from this year of 2004 offers insight into why I express this sentiment, and how the beliefs had been changed in 1000 BCE.

Excerpts from Book 4 of the Denkard

I make obeisance to Mazda-worshipping religion which is opposed to the demons (and) is the ordinance of Ohrmazda. The matter of the fourth book (of the Denkard) is composed from sentences selected from Ayinin Amuk Vazin by Adurfarnbag, I Farroxzadan, the leader of the faith of the family of the educated-in-the-faith, and saintly Adarbad Mahraspandan.

Be it known that the one God is the cause of the beginning (of creation) and is the causer of causes. Cause is not for him (i.e. He is uncaused.)

Among those connected with (God) the second as the second (if we regard Ohrmazda as the first), (and) first among the original creation is Vohuman. The commencement of creation was with Vohuman.

And the origin adverse to him (i.e. Vohuman's adversary) is (Ahriman) the blemish giving cause of the creation.

Seeing with complete vision (i.e. on careful inquiry) it is found that the other with the perverse understanding (i.e. Ahriman) conducts things in this world (in the path of evil). At times several original (creations) are destroyed through him. Because his creation separates itself from those who have a close connection with their original master (i.e. God) have taken the side of his adversary. In addition, it is becoming unfit by not caring to keep up with their connection with their true god and by harming the moderate party (of God) it is broken (from its own party). For the same reason that substance, which is on the adverse side of harming the side (of god) is not fit to receive the gifts (of God). Again, a substance, which has received its life from the one life-giving God, becomes unfortunate through the same cause. Any person who turns against Him from whom he got his birth is not able to improve himself (morally) through his connection with that one (i.e. Ahriman), because he is connected with his (i.e. Ahriman's) substance.

Again that evil one is not, as the creation of Vohuman is, the second creation of God. From this it appears that the great self-existing God who is a law unto Himself is one and alone.

And from one (creation) after another is created by him. Hence no one else can be his equal as an adversary (i.e. Ahriman can never equal Him). The one God is he who through that one (i.e., Vohuman) has given birth to innumerable other creations.

The creation connected with that other (i.e. Ahriman) is without religion; how can it be said to have connection with the second (creation, viz. Vohuman)? But that one (i.e. the creation connected with Ahriman) this can be said to be separated from the One (God).

Third-- The creation-increasing origin (i.e. God) keeps the second (creation) Ardwahisht under the supervision of one who is among those connected with Him (i.e. under Vohuman). Among the Amahraspands, Ardwahisht has the third rank. And he is obedient to the first creation (Vohuman). The reason of this being third (in rank) is that Ohrmazda he is the first and as being the first creation, Vohuman is the second (in rank), and his (i.e. Vohuman's) obedient servants Ardwahisht are considered the third (in rank). From this, Vohuman having obtained his life from Ohrmazda is (Ohrmazda's) obedient servant. And the good custom and law of (men) obeying the authority of Ohrmazda and of living as His obedient servants has (prevailed in the world) from the beginning of creation through the THOUGHT of (Vohuman). Again the good custom of life- possessing men publicly obeying and respecting religious rulers is (prevailing in the world through Vohuman).

Among those connected with the perfect authority of Ohrmazda the fourth in rank called Shahrewar is worthy of being blessed through his possessing life according to Ohrmazda. And he is a worthy servant of the worker of pure deeds, Ardwahisht. And this second (creation, Ardwahisht) is obedient to Vohuman the first creation. (Shahrewar presides over metals. In addition, these give strength for generosity and nourishment to men living a life of piety. Thereby is (acquisition of) honor, (attainment of) one's desires, propagation of the faith, attainment of (both) knowledge and the intuitive wisdom of the good-thought Vohuman. Thereby is the springing up (in the heart) of the desire of obedience to God, the conducting of oneself towards Ardwahisht to one's (own) advantage, and the making one's friends do likewise. To conduct the people by the authority of Ohrmazda and the leadership of the faith is to disgrace the blemish-giver (Ahriman). And hence the blessed are exalted.

Again he who keeps up the divine religion in this world and rules the people according to the precepts of religion is the (king or priest) the maintainer or religion and of the true and temperate authority of God.

The state through the (inspired) strength of the knowledge of religion is worthy of the trust (of the people) and those who in truth and purity propagate the knowledge of religion among the pious are strong through the strength of the state.

Ungodliness and the intense prevalence of unholy utterances (in state and church) are through the rival efforts of the adversary (i.e. Ahriman) to (keep himself) in touch (with men). In the same way the method of (men's) speech and deeds is like unto fire. Just as burning fire (first) dries up the wet firewood and (next) after drying up the firewood acknowledges the ruddy light (akin to itself), so too in both ways (i.e. the two referred to above) the people of the world by their holiness are fit to drive away the unholy Druj from among them (i.e. the fire first expels the adverse principle of water from the wet fuel so too piety first drives out the unholy element; next the fire makes the fuel glowing hot and absorbs the fuel into itself and so too piety absorbs that which remains after the unholy element has been driven off and makes akin to itself). It behooves the people to acknowledge these obligations to the agents (i.e. the Mobeds and Dasturs) who give them an insight into the nature of the different kinds of Unholiness and those who give rise to different sorts of harms. In the same manner people ought to be always extremely grateful to the good triumphant kings, the defenders of the faith. Because he (i.e. such a king) is the believer in the religion loved of God and more especially because he explains the wisdom underlying the Mazda-worshipping faith. Hence his good Government is safe and permanent. And by the adornment derived from his and the Yazad's mutual connection he is secretly sheltered (and protected). And the continuance of his authority one after the other (in his own family) is through divine assistance. Therefore, people should look upon the religious kings who have faith in their religion as courageous, as being the good kings of religion and the kings who are of the law of the (good) faith should attempt to spread in the world the exalted law-abiding wisdom of the Mazda-worshipping faith.

When king Vishtasp became relieved from the war with Arjasp, he sent messages to other kings to accept the (Mazda-worshipping) faith and to spread). Among the people) the writings of the Mazda-worshipping religion which are studded with all wisdom and which relate to the acquisition of knowledge and resources of various kinds, he sent all together (i.e. at the same time). Spiti, Arezrasp and other Mobeds who had studied the languages relating to these (writings) and who had returned from Khwaniras [Xwaniratha] after a complete study of the knowledge of the faith under Frashostar.

Darai son of Darai ordered the preservation of two written copies of the whole *Avesta* and its commentary according as it was accepted by Zartosht, from Ohrmazda, one in the Ganj-i-hapigan and the other in the Dez-i-Napesht.

The Ashkanian government got the *Avesta* and its commentary, which from its (original) pure (and sound) condition had been, owing to the devastation and harm (inflicted by) Alexander and his general of the plundering Ahriman army, separated into parts and scattered about, to be copied out. And any (work) which remained with the Dasturs for there study and the writings subsequently obtained in the city were ordered to be preserved and copies of them to be made out for other cities.

(After this) Ardashir-i-Papakan in his time got a true Dastur named Tosar to arrange together all the scattered writings relating to the *Avesta* and its commentaries. For this (order) Dastur Tosar devoting his attention to (this subject) made one harmonious work after comparison with other writings. He entrusted the Dasturs with the work of making other copies of it. The king also ordered that other writings relating to the Mazda-worshipping faith with might be obtained after him and of which no information or clue was to be had then should be preserved in the same way.

Shahpuhr son of Ardashir king of kings collected together, from Hindustan, Arum and other places where they had got scattered, writings other than those of the faith (i.e. other than those on prayer, worship, precepts, and law), (such as) those relating to medicine, astronomy, geography, minerals, the increase of the glory of life-possessing kinds, the parts of the soul, and (writings relating to) other arts and sciences.

And he ordered a correct copy of them after collocation with the *Avesta* to be deposited in the Ganj-i-Shaspigan. And he ordered the (Dasturs and Mobeds) to deliver sermons and speeches to draw the faith of the people without religion to the Mazda-worshipping faith.

Shahpuhr king of kings, son of Ohrmazda warred with the kings of all countries and made them believers in Ohrmazda. And he created a taste (for religion) among all people by means of speeches. And he made them investigators of religion. And at last Adarbad by his admonitions made the people high priest placed before all the non-Zoroastrians an explanation of all the different Nasks of the *Avesta*. Upon which some who accepted the faith confessed to this effect-- we have seen with our eyes every point of the faith and hence every one of us is sure to abandon his evil religion, and we shall keep up our efforts for the faith. And they did accordingly.

Now Khosraw, king of kings, son of Kobad drove out from among the four divisions of (the people of) the faith (i.e. from the Athonrnan, Artheshtar, Vastriosh and Hutokhsh) any priest of the evil religion and ruler of the evil religion who seemed to be full of enmity to the faith, (in fact he drove out) all these evil men. And he has exalted the Zoroastrians (through their faith) by giving them from time to time encouragement and instruction regarding the faith.

Again (Khosraw) has given this order about the (priests gifted with) divine wisdom -- that the clever men who explain the truth of the Mazda-worshipping faith should through their good judgment and foresight encourage the ignorant by teaching them the faith and make them as steadfast as possible in their faith. And the learned supreme high priest, the Dastur of the Dasturs should not enter into religious discussion with the people. But he should through pure thought, word, and deed is on the side of the good spirits. And he should piously worship and pray to God through the Manthras that by (his) worshipping with the Manthras we might always call to our mind the leader of our people *i.e.* of the Magus to wit Ohrmazda; The Lord (God) is manifest unto us through spiritual understanding. And the Lord shows us through spiritual **THOUGHT** the measures for our salvation so as to be understood of us of the world. We will continue to love Him fully from among the Yazads by both the agencies (of the spiritual and bodily faculties). Moreover, we will continue to remember the Yazads who work for the prosperity of God's world in order that religious merit might accrue to those of the good faith.

Again, that king (i.e. Khosraw) in an addition to this (work) sent the inhabitants of Iran studding the Mazda-worshipping faith to Khwaniras to study under teachers of exalted wisdom, so that we might acquire full adornment through knowledge of the divine religion. These keep aloof from perverse discussions, exhort (men to lead a good life) through the words of the Avesta and compose books of wisdom. And people through their wise writings keep themselves moderate and honored by obeying those who enlighten them. Again for this reason all men regard the Mazda-worshipping faith of divine wisdom as meant for the final existence. Hence intellectual strangers continue coming to this place (i.e. Iran) for (studying) the Ohrmazda-worshipping divine religion. Explanation of the Mazda- worshipping faith is afforded to people from the outside that continue coming to obtain connection with and zeal for the new religion. And the Dasturs after many (religious) researches with still greater zeal travel and instruct those who cannot come there (i.e. to Iran) for the work of obtaining the benefit of the faith.

Again (Khosraw) thus addressed all the Mobeds who are evidently servants of God and of virtuous disposition -- I order you with the best wish (i.e. most sincerely) that you should create a taste for the Avesta and its exposition [Zand] with new and new zeal. And by the acquisition of its knowledge (i.e. of the Avesta) the worthy people of the world should be made exalted in rank. They should fully instruct such, as are capable of learning, from among the people of the world, who do not understand the Creator, nor the details regarding his miraculous spiritual creation. Such as are wanting in intelligence and are of perverse THOUGHTS should be instructed in the faith in way that seems best, to wit, by comparisons (and examples) and be who can instruct (people) in the faith with such wisdom should be regarded as the instructing (priest).

The profession of that instructor in the faith, who is a teacher fit for the above (work), who has spiritual gifts, who instructs (men) in every wisdom of the faith and who likewise plainly tells with wisdom the vices of the world to every one, is the only one which makes men (incline) to the divine faith. He should not expound anything on the authority of the faith, which is not in agreement with the exposition of the faith. Likewise he should teach on the authority of the faith everything that is found in the faith as a duty he owes to his office.

(The Creator Ohrmazda) for (the maintenance of) His authority produced and gave being to the increase-giving Spandarmad of obedient thought, the fifth among his holy relatives. This is the begetting power for begetting spiritual and earthy creation (in the world). Through Spandarmad is the strength of the earthy body, the sense of feeling, courage and every kind of foresight. Man is obedient to God and possessing His glory on account of the presence in him of thought, word, and deed, which makes him obedient to God. For in pious men is the lodgment of the Yazads for the complete recompense of virtue and the presence of the Yazads vanishes (from among men) because of their connection with impiety. Moreover in men is the relation of exalting foresight and five other substances (life, soul, intellect, conscience, and guarding spirit) whose names are mentioned in religion.

Ohrmazda created among (His) relatives (i.e. the Archangels [Amahraspands]) the essence of (archangel) Hordad sixth in high dignity, always bestowing gifts and endowed with the thought of obedience. This creation on account of its communion with many earthy substances (especially time and water) yields good thought to the good creation in its allotted work, takes proper care of it, as a faith companion keeps itself in communion with the essence of (the good creation,) and out of the feeling of kinship keeps itself united with (the good creation) to show it the full and proper path in every work and process. In the same manner, the hidden qualities, which are with Hordad -- viz., the resplendent Farohar, conscience, life, intelligence, wisdom, and others pertaining to the affairs of the soul, -- remain as the corrector and manager of the body. The invisible physical senses give intimation unto the soul, of sinful actions, which the body commits with regard to the soul. These invisible (senses) are called the mediators between body and soul. Moreover, these senses yield happiness to both bodies bad souls by making these two assist each other.

The seventh (related to Ohrmazda) is (the Archangel) Amurdad, which, besides yielding protection unto men, always keeps living men immortal and connected with the (faithful) flock. He is the promoter of thoughtful, meditating nature, bestowed of progeny to the warriors, and begetter of good thought among those who are born. He yields radiance to the bodies of those who are bore good and is of many natures through the mingling of wisdom.

The one existence of God perfects and completes itself in seven (including the sixth spiritual archangels.) It befits all to thank God for perfection in all deed. (As every nature obtains capacity to enjoy life) and for being engaged in their proper work. God gets victory (over Ahriman) through the thanks given unto Him by the creatures for being able to occupy themselves in their proper work. This thanksgiving (from men) is due on account of the nature they have received from Him (i.e. on account of the useful life obtained from Him.)

Learned archpriests must impart knowledge of religion to the creatures of God. From the scholars of the Manthras-utterances well versed in religion is attained a, proper understanding of the industry each man ought to engage in and of the way he should work.

The creatures are not informed as regards the infinite time connected with God, its nature being understood only by the unique existence (i.e.) the Creator himself.

The creation of finite time on earth is for (bringing about) the improvement of the creatures having existence by means of a change from one (condition) to another (the change being from the material world, into which man is born from the spiritual, back into the spiritual state.) As regards the cause of creation) it is said in religion that every one comes into being from Him who has being (i.e. God) and every creature that is created obtains existence from that existent (i.e. God.)

The utterances of God (i.e. the sayings of the Mazdayasnian religion) are a law unto the existing (i.e. to men.) There is nothing without order. Some of the substances are finite. Moreover the substance wanting in order is from the blemish giver (i.e. is on the side of Ahriman,) and is said to be the substance following the law of wicked similitude. (I.e. of Ahriman) and existing without rule and limit (i.e. without the restriction of law.) Just as the period of the Creator's existence is infinite so is the exalted soul; how can it (ever) have non-existence?

The creation, which is produced, receives by its actions gifts of a high order from God.

Moreover, men perform meritorious actions because of fate or destiny and it is this account of (destiny) that a being of the earth is considered famous among the spiritual Yazads. Through the performance of actions pertaining to the spiritual world is man's high destiny. In this world, a man of greatness receives the favor of God so long as he has faith in the shining Yazads. In the same manner a man following the reverse path turns to meanness and degradation through worldliness. The good thought power Vohuman that gives light to the eye (i.e. the understanding) of man is (obtained) by loving the powerful wealth (i.e. course of life), which makes for improvement. He who is without this wealth is without the above-mentioned things (for the improvement of wisdom.)

Men ought to raise themselves to illustrious positions by worldly knowledge and by education (which enables them) to read and write. They should keep themselves with the bounds of law and order by the precepts of the faith and purchase many books containing wise sayings. For obtaining immortality (in the next world) they should duly praise the helping Yazads and struggle with (the wicked.) Many virtuous men improve and exalt the one substance (i.e. the soul) by praising the Yazads. (The arch-priests) explain to the people the nature of the several (wicked beings) who are always for quarrel, inimical to the creations of (Ohrmazda) and helpful to the creatures of darkness

(Men) ought to acknowledge they are the giver of existence the Creator who endowed living men with bodies possessing complete supremacy with the help of fire and water.

Those who do not turn to the faith of the Daevas (i.e. those who cling to the religion of Mazda-worship with firm faith) must be rewarded. Those who lead mankind with the intention of making them recognize one God must be made the governors of the world, and those who keep to the mandates of religion must be called (men) of pure origin. In the same manner the contemplators of Divine knowledge must be rewarded with such gifts, as they desire.

Things which are fit to be supplied at some place for (keeping up) the existence (of animated beings) must be most certainly borne there in any way (that is possible;) as for instance, the water of the river which gives strength to life, and medicine prepared in cold and warm water for (removing) discomfort from the soul (both in life and at the time of death.) It is the good thoughtful (physician) that knows the proper medicine for (giving) blood, shining (complexion), consciousness, and taste.

Just as the Flame is through live fire, light through flame, and twilight after light, in the same manner, the greater or less recovery (of animate beings) from many a disease, takes place by means of medicinal herbs.

Just as the date tree grows up from the date-stone, in the same manner the production of man is through the act of procreation.

For the connection of progeny (i.e. for begetting offspring) the sexual congress of one person with another is (essential.)

Permanence of life depends on the soul's connection with the body.

Rain or the Yazads bestowing rain are the cause of prosperity to living beings.

The permanence of friendship and amity is through seeing and conversing with one another.

How is existence brought about? Just as one substance is evolved out of another according to its own laws and in the finite time (fixed for it.)

What the produce of a certain city is, or what grows up in its lands is understood by knowledge of (the city.)

The first gift of life-giving Creator is as regards the soul. The students of the Manthras properly understand the different gifts relating to the soul, bestowed by the Creator. Nor are the proper remedies for the last pangs of the soul hidden from them.

Questions:
The following are the questions of those who retail scandal against honest religious beliefs.

Q. Is the potent being (God) finite or not?

A. The answer is this that the leader of religion (the chief arch-priest) remains glorious by receiving God's halo of exalted worth. In the same manner he is the agent (of God) to encourage people to perform works of religion by means of his far-seeing understanding. Therefore by actions unworthy of a leader he does not lose his previously obtained position as a leader of religion.

Q. Is the potent being (God) capable of wisdom to a limited extent or more the (i.e. is He omniscient or not?)

A. The star-readers (i.e. astrologers) understand the worth of the allotment (of destiny by the stars).

How long is the chief allotting (stars) to move in bad aspects? How long are they in conjunction with the malignant owner of bad aspects? How long does the man (influenced by such stars) work in the way of wisdom? The laws relating to these and other (astrological) details the astrologers learn from writings on the earth (i.e. from astrology). Astrologers can foretell the good events of a man's (life) from his horoscope. And physicians can explain the details (regarding the health of the body, the safety of the body and the connection of the soul with the body. Those who are connected (with a man) infer from his outward movements his life, the destruction of his life, his actions and his investigations. Knowledge of the substances and of the creation of time and place is (attained) by (the explanation of) the creator (i.e. by inspiration.) Through the nature (of the substance) is (attained) the knowledge of its qualities and through creation its existence (is known). Knowledge of perverse substances is attained through understanding the nature of acceptable substances.

Q. Does (God) irradiate His glory through intermediaries?

A. The obedient soul (created by) the Almighty is so on account of the connection and radiance of the immortal (Yazads) whose knowledge the holy God has bestowed on (the obedient soul). With the blessing of that radiance that (man) becomes famous by performing every earthly action according to his will. And through unanimity with the opponent (Ganamino) man prevents his nature (from virtuous actions). And he who completely reforms the different natures of the adversary's (connections) renders himself fortunate. His progeny keeps to the original (nature from which he is sprung). The race of horses is (sprung up) from the first horse; the production of orange is from the first orange tree. In the same manner, that a man should completely improve his progeny, for its safety and continuance, is necessary for making his race famous.

Through abiding by the mandates of God observing the precepts of religion on earth the soul of man and his progeny acquire an insight into the things relative to the good creation (i.e. the spiritual world), eternal wisdom and (eternal) time (as naturally as) the eye (acquires) the power of vision. By means of this every nature keeps his material existence connected with God, in the same manner as twilight is connected with light.

The religious governor conversant with religion is a great instrument, for the worship and praise of God.

Firstly-- (The king) must be susceptible of beneficent wisdom, and useful to those related with him. Secondly -- The king is supposed to pay respect to worthy beings (i.e. men walking in the path of God). Thirdly-- (The king) is supposed to be without deviation from divine mandates, fulfilling God's wish, and is reckoned superior through (possessing) God's wisdom. Fourthly -- (The king) does not become supreme by disowning the superiority of the potent Yazads, but is supposed to perform other dishonest actions, through adverse intentions. (The king) who deals justice, according to the precepts of God's revelation, has an effective remedy for the grief's of the people of this world and keeps his subjects well off by means of justice. That the (king) preserves his dignity with permanent fame by means of these (his) actions, (which are) without harm and bring on prosperity. It behooves the King to inflict on men two kinds of punishment for their offenses in order to establish his fame. The one (punishment) is bodily (i.e. giving physical labor to the body) and the other is the infliction of fine. The sage judges, studying the Manthras, know every kind of punishment. The man under the dominion of (the demons) the instructors of sins declares (in a court of justice) that he is a witness, and gives harmful evidence, in spite of not seeing (anything). How can that man receive salvation from the sin of unfaithfulness? The students of justice discern the (real) thoughts of these men of (wicked) connection, on account of the lodgment of the Yazads among them, (which lodgment is) like the lodgment of water in clay. The connection of adverse (i.e. unjust) judges is harmful (to the Yazads); therefore they are regarded as not connected (with the Yazads). For this it reasons the substance under the dominion of the Yazads is considered to be of exalted (i.e. supernal) existence, and the substance not under their dominion is called (the thing) of darkness (infernal) and non-existence. Again, the substance under the dominion of (Ganamino) the despoiler of existence enjoys the (wicked) existence of its master. The substance possessing the wisdom of the Yazads acts in the creation, just like an effulgent supernal power. And so long as the substance during its life does not excite (itself) (with Ahriman's power), it is said to be of proper connection. In addition, those men of whom Yazads are supposed to be the masters are the servants of God, enjoying His favor; harm cannot reach them.

Q. If the potent being (God) were infinite, how can He be called potent being? Again how can one possessing finite power be called the potent being?

A. (In reply to the questions: Has God who is worthily of (eternal) existence any limit? and in knowledge is He capable to a certain extent or is His capability beyond limit?) The explanation therefore is that God has concern with finite time, and is Lord of finite knowledge, but He being (himself) without limit as to knowledge and time, is said to be of unlimited time and unlimited knowledge.

Q. Should all works be done at their proper (i.e. destined) time? Can they be done at other times? Can a work be without reward?

A. (Is there any transmission of Light from one to another? The answer to which is that) the God of Existence is the best leader (of the world temporal and spiritual) and He is capable of imparting His own Light to another.

Q. Are all works done at present in accord with know-ledge and wisdom? If a work is connected with the original strength (i.e. has come from the source of goodness, God) how can it be said in light of the faith to belong to infinite time?

A. To the people who have existence God, through his chief creation through the good-thinking angelic power grivet a comprehension of the end of their creation.

Q. How can the leader of darkness be truthful? Who leads the true leader astray?

A. Those that are dwellers in Hell have been mentioned as (inmates) of Darkness, not of Light. Whatever elements there are of heat, cold, moisture, and dryness in the bodies of those (i.e. men) living as the companions of the Yazads, they have been created (by God) for doing the work of the body. They thus serve to keep in good order the vitality and are the means of keeping the body sound.

In the same way (evil agencies) that do harm (to the body) cause the elements of cold and dryness to dwell in the body, and permeate the human system to the injury of the elements of the heat and moisture that do the work of vivifying the body. The coexistence of these four elements in equitable relations with each other tends to the amelioration of the body.

Q. How does the life-giver (God) give outward form (to all substances?)?

A. Unfair and defective agencies cause harm to the body. The Life-giving One (God) is not sustainer of the adverse creation. All men oppose, obstruct, and fight with one another for the existence of the principle with which they are connected (i.e. are either for Spenamino or Ganamino). Nay, the different opponents who fully grace the principle to which they belong are related to their kind (i.e. to the side to which each has given his choice). Thus a thing of cold (essence) is known to suppress heat, and a thing of dry (essence) to suppress moisture. When the representative of one side encounters the representative of the other, it is not for suppressing him altogether, but with the motive of obstructing, the work assigned to him by (natural) Law. The uniform state of the blood is due to the dryness, which is related, to heat and moisture, which is related to cold. In the same way an organic body is rendered unfit when heat accompanies moisture, and cold accompanies dryness; the blood stops in consequence, and at once flows in the opposite direction. As the sources of the elements bring about dryness connected with heat, and moisture connected with cold, there is much a commingling of heat with cold and of dryness with moisture, that this relation being kept up in the body, it conduces to the proper animation of the same, and the body always remains busy at its work along with the connected Yazads. All misunderstandings and quarrels, which now occur at times between individuals, are due to the related influences becoming unworthy. This is brought about by the lower existences (i.e. the evil powers of the demons) commingling in the body. When those of one kind make a sudden attempt to make the body unfit, it is brought into affinity with death. And the ruin of the body is through its being enfeebled in many ways by destructive evil tendencies. Also the Spirit that is opposed to the vital action of the body is the (invisible) one that tries to make the body act contrary to uniform laws. The man works for good life of his body through the spiritual powers, which work for his (virtuous) existence. The cessation of the work of existence, pertaining to the good recompense of the soul, is due to the body becoming lightless (i.e. lifeless), by the development of the work of the destructive forces (in the body) the enfeebling powers therein are strengthened. The good bright Yazads that have relation with men keep them from contact with the adverse forces (i.e. the demons). <u>It is mentioned in the religious books that it is through the influence of the spiritually existing Yazads residing in men, that they (men) are free from various kinds of harm and evil.</u>

Q. How can the faithful of this world perform actions the aim and object of which would be the same as (the aim and object) of (the Yazads and Amahraspands) the radiant being that always carry out God's wishes?

A. Again, among the various professions the choicest is that of the heads of the religion, and the one pertaining to the attainment of the love of the Yazads, and that of loading oneself to the performance of noble actions in this, world.

Q. In what ways is the worshipper of God distinct from the one who scorns Him? Why should one who has power of endurance complain (against pain?)? How can a substance become very famous?

A. The knowledge of what man's duties are and what they are not is acquired by man through there being a sufficient number of the family of the religious leaders (i.e. through there being a sufficient number of Dasturs and Mobeds informed in religion), who are the ardent (i.e. careful) preservers of the Avesta an its commentaries. And they are thus the expounders of the religion in public to the people of the world, the instructors of the philosophy of the Religion to the people, and proclaim of the (religious) truth to those that argue perversely against it. They are those that embarrass all famine-producers and ravagers of fertility. <u>They are those that attract people to the worship of God, and make them obey their kings and honor the decisions of their judges.</u> They are those that make the people of the four divisions (the Athonrnan, the Artheshtar, the Vastriosh and the Hutokhsh) illustrious in their respective occupations. In addition, by means have Questions and answers pertaining to Ohrmazda, they make them devoted to religion, students of religion, and worshippers of God. They keep in currency the requirements other the other Athonrnan, (i.e. they supply them the things they want), and fulfill their wishes, whereby good and respectable families are maintained honorably. Those (men) that are the instructors in the Zartosht [Zoroastrian] religion are the promoters of the desire for religion and the disseminators of the knowledge of it. The other thing pertaining to the Mazdayasnian faith, (i.e. wisdom), which, in so far as it serves the purpose of clearing up all misunderstanding (i.e. doubts), is pleasing to those that tread the path of God, is to be kept pure. And the new seekers after knowledge must, by being put in the way of acquiring it, are kept above want. In him that does not advance his community, and forbids not men from immoral acts, good faith should not be placed. And he should never be regarded as a leader (of the community) or as one who can remove the apprehensions of each individual, or as one who can make the other creation (i.e. the atheists) obedient to God.

Through repentance of sin is attainable the receiving go the recompense for righteousness and the discarding of sin. And after that there is no occasion for punishment. Connection with the med for a single act of righteousness is the cause of the reduction of the punishment for the sins (of that man). It is God's object to make those, who disobey the commands of the king, deserving of various kinds of punishments by way of justice. Among them, the one who disobeys the commands (of the king), and the one who is imprisoned for all the offenses relating to the soul, are to be released by order of the State. In addition, if a prisoner has been put in imprisonment by recourse to ways contrary to orders, (i.e. in contravention of the laws of justice), for causing grievous wrong to the soul, it is a kind of oppression. Again, at the bidding of the physician that heals the disorders of the soul (i.e. the Dasturs of the religion), it would be conformable to religion to let off a highwayman from capital punishment.

Q. The Sun shines on the earth according to the time of the season, Why are (then) some places without the heat of the illuminator? Although (substances) improve by means of the illuminating Sun, some places are (even) at noontide moist and dirty. Why should it be that one place is moist in spite of the noonday heat whereas another gets more than its portion of the light of the Sun?

Q. How is the inability to look at the effulgent light (of the Sun to be explained?)? Why is the weakening and enfeebling of the eyesight thereby? How can pain proceed from the luminous Sun, which derives its power from God?

A. For the leaders of the world -- those that are crowned with supreme majesty (i.e. the king and the Dasturs) -- the equitable Government of iranshehr is feasible through illustrious judges -- the dispensers of justice. The maintenance of the sovereignty over the seven regions by the Zoroastrians is due to there being an abode within them of Religion, the Kayanian majesty, and other glories. Again, the means that they have for living in exuberance (i.e. in comfort), and the cause of all their pristine greatness and supremacy are due to their having within them the coming and going of the Yazads (i.e. to their intercourse with the Yazads and Amahraspands). And it is on account of this very sovereignty (endowed with Yazads majesty) that such a king of Iran is able to invest with power the rulers of the seven regions. As the flame of a fire is due to its relation with the inward glow, and as light is due to its relation with the flame, in the same manner is Wisdom due to Religion, and superior power is attainable (by man) by his relation with the instructor of the Religion. And through an insight into (i.e. comprehension of) it is the (righteous) existence of man. And through his connection with the open path (of religion) is the test (of man). And through such power (of religious wisdom) is the body able to perform the functions necessary to the soul. And through soundness of the body is the preservation of the soul. All Iranians (i.e. Mazdayasnian) by so regulating themselves can live with a superior kind of strength. Those of the citizens that give instruction in (the acquirement of) knowledge, spiritual forces, art, courage, physical strength, and prosperity, make the rule of the king of Iran supreme, auspicious, and honored.

    The greatness of the Iranians (i.e. the Mazdayasnian) is owing to truthfulness in all matters, kind regard, and meditation on the design of Providence in all-powerful creations. By these means, they keep in affinity to their source (i.e. their Creator), and obtain victory over men of the opposite nature and over the ignoble and wild-looking subject nations of other cities. Again the Mazdayasnian should give good advice to the people that are of harsh and abominable traits, evil-worshippers, and enfeebled, so that these may not waste their life in vain actions. And they should form men, who are not of good essence (i.e. are evil), into being good men, like the present good-thinking pious men, who are particularly careful in their adherence to noble speech and in keeping aloof from base things.

Had not the people of the good Creation put themselves at first into an awkward position before the rulers, by the use of (inept) expressions, they would never have become, but could have remained with their faculties on alert. In addition, had they not in this way come to disregard the divine commands, and to deprive themselves of the intellect guarded over by the Yazads, they would have been able to understand what things are to be done and what not to be done. And they would have known that the Yazads effulgence of the luminous soul couldn't for long dwell in the body just as the sun refrains from making luminous (for all time) the good things that shine by the sun's light. (The Yazads radiance) it has been known to interrupt by the man's being very careless. Therefore it is that for certain reasons contradictory words should not be uttered in the presence of rulers; and in order to keep oneself in good repute one should, in their presence, give expression to one's THOUGHS after mature consideration.

Premeditation is necessary in questioning and in answering, and then the question may be put, or the reply given, in the proper way. It is the way of the priests of the false religions not to act with good sense, before they are overpowered.

Q. Do the Yazads guarding the earth give up the work of man's salvation, through fear of the wicked?

A. Before putting a question in one's turn, one should catch the drift of the opponent's argument. Again, in a discussion, he that speaks much should not be checked, but his reasoning should be well listened to. Also, in a discussion, if there be a question, it should be satisfactorily answered. If there be many such questions they should be dealt with in various ways.

The perfect glory (i.e. the Divine gift) that fits men for leadership is of the nature, viz. that such people take upon themselves to answer properly the questions of those that argue well; but he that has faculty for (mere) fault such a disputant does not argue for self-improvement. Nor is his discussion pertaining to the soul, and therefore such discussion should be dropped. The discussion which is beneficial, and pertaining to the salvation (of the soul) from Hell, and for the welfare of the soul, should not be set aside, but should be carried out to the solution. Nor should one refrain from exposing falsehood, wrong ideas, and wickedness. To secure their deliverance from Hell, they (the people) should be led, by all kinds of truth, to have implicit and unshaken faith; and from this there should be no turning aside for whatsoever reason. And like the spring season one should show himself at his best in his ardor (for expounding the religion). If the signification of anything (pertaining to religion) were not clear, it should be given out as unintelligible. And in the argument whatever is worth esteeming should be appreciated in detail Moreover, no wrong deed that might have been done should be admired. But the right action only that has been per-formed by the help of God should be accepted as beneficial.

The foremost leader of the religion (i.e. the Dasturan Dastur [Zarathushtrotema]) should imbue the people with ardor for the religion, and should induce them to be very industrious, in order to make them excel in their routine of work, and should exhort them to acquire other noble arts.

Those that have been in touch with the Yazads (viz. the believing Mazdayasnian), should, by girding themselves for the fight, making use of the right understanding (about Spenamino and Ganamino), ward off one of them (the Ganamino), and follow the other (the Spenamino). And with the strength and courage derived from the Spenamino they should attack the other (Ganamino), and (by the help of the Spenamino) they should obtain the nourishment of their nature. Till the end, the fight should be maintained with Ganamino, who should never be regarded as having received good training.

Q. How can the expelled Blemish-giver be (present) in him who is innocent? If God should recompense them and make them of great worth how can the truthful ever think of sorrow and the charitable bestowals of corn [i.e. grain] ever suffer from hunger?

A. The charitable man is he who bestows in charity from his own (acquired) wealth. And the truthful man is he who never speaks untruth on behalf of or about another person.

The grateful man is he who recognizes an obligation. Gratitude should be shown towards him to whom one, like a dependant, is under obligation for his life. And, secondly, gratitude should be shown towards him who having the power to harm hath done no harm; and finally, when one has experienced all possible good from him, one must assuredly show one's gratitude by words and deeds.

Those that are engaged in the inquiry (i.e. search) after immortality, acceptable to God, and (are the friends) of the benevolent (i.e. the imparters of religious instruction), and of other benefactors, are the procurers of other felicities for their kith and kin; and by not bearing any ill-feeling towards robbers and other harm-doers, towards prisoners, and other criminals and wretched people, and by making them happy and faithful, they prove themselves possessors of the good strength worth being grateful for (i.e. Those who showing compassion towards robbers, prisoners, and sinners, lead them to improvement, really bring them under their obligation by making them staunch believers (in the faith). But by cherishing hatred towards them they are held to be in danger of becoming guilty.

A father ought to reform his son, if he were unworthily, by inculcating in him noble thoughts (i.e. by religious instruction). Therefore, if a man from want of assistance were incapable of doing any work, he should, in order that he may surmount all kinds of wretchedness, be given the means to acquire more wealth.

Q. People consider the evidence of (persons) of high descent as throwing more light than that, of untrue speakers; but why should they be considered of high descent and lofty dignity if they serve the will of sovereigns of low worth. One whom God has declared to be of (royal) family in the Avesta is not to be considered royal. But if (such a person) serve not the will of wicked sovereigns should his royal descent be acknowledged?

A. A discussion on religion may be entered into with those of the controversialists on religious subjects, who are so (learned) as to be able to give authoritative decision on all subjects. Thus the truth on their side being known, they may have no occasion on punish, according to the dictates of the Nasks (of the Avesta), the priests of the false religion.

A certain nation's scriptures, known by the name of True [Torah] (i.e. the scriptures of the Jews viz. the Torat or the Injil) have been regarded as the words of the devils, and are not worthy of belief. Nothing mentioned therein deserves to be done for the benefit of the creation. Because the writing makes mention of the irrelevant matters which ought not to have been introduced therein. Whatever therein is not good writing is the concoction of various writers, and therefore such writings is said to be of the soul-cramping tendency. And these concocted accounts the Jews regards the revelation of the original creation (i.e. pertaining to the celestial Yazads).

To the Rummies who help the Yazdan-worshippers of good wisdom (i.e. who help those of the Mazdayasnian faith) and to others who live a similar (good) life, should be expounded the original text of the 'Ganj-i-Shaspigan.' (In other words, the Jews and the Greeks who whish to believe in the Mazdayasnian religion), and such of them as have no faith in their own, and want to improve, should be thoroughly instructed in the religion.

If in other countries there be any writings (respecting our religion) worth reading, new, ameliorating, good, and divinely inspired, these should be procured; and there should be no backwardness in the study of them and in the researches into them. And whatever in the writings of other nations is unbelievable should not be accepted.

The nature that has concern with the greatest development of wisdom (i.e. is studious) must be admired. Attention should be given to the writings of (the men of) other countries, and the same should not be destroyed.

In these writings (of men of other countries) if there be any passages and aphorisms pertaining to the service of the one God. It is not every comment thereon or every maxim that is to be indiscriminately given publicity out of the body of those writings and maxims; but we should make from them a selection of the original (sacred) passages and maxims (pertaining to our religion). And the books in the Ganj-i-Shaspigan should be read with careful attention to all the passages.

In these writings (i.e. those pertaining to our religion) the human body is treated of in four parts, of which the head is said to be presided over by the Athornan (i.e. the priestly) class, and the hand by the Artheshtar (i.e. the warrior) class, the stomach by the agricultural class, and the leg by the people who follow good avocations for livelihood.

The human soul is said to have the chief control over all the above-mentioned four classes, and the soul itself is said to be under the dominion of God.

A twofold object evidently influences the words and deeds of every man. His first object is to qualify himself for the final (welfare), and his second object is to endow himself with noble thoughts by so training himself for the profession (of piety.)

The Iranians (i.e. the God-fearing Mazdayasnians) are deserving of praise because of all their honest dealings, while dishonest and blemish men deserve to be condemned.

The celebrated erudite Seneca's of Rum, and the servants of India have shown an appreciation of and have much admired the foresighted persons of Iran. They adopted their expressions and ideas, and on seeing the great worth of these wise men of Iran showed their preference for them.

Q. How can the Emperor Ardashir Papakan's sovereignty be acknowledged in spite of the severance of authority from several of his direct ancestors?

For the same reason many scholars became worthy to obtain high position and favor from the (Iranian) rulers. And by obtaining high recompense and support (from the Iranian leaders), they in order to get a full reward of their merit, much dreaded these leaders in this world, and were much afraid of punishment in the next. Moreover, they abstained from these blemishes, so that they might continue (to receive) honest recompense from their Iranian superiors who could hold them back (from such blemishes.)

And they themselves, (i.e. the leaders), in their desire to obtain a good recompense for their souls, abstained from any carelessness that might cause them to be miserable in the abode or palace, village or city of the next world; arid they never gave way to any lustful passion. However, they cherished the learned men, with the view of securing distinction as men of worth. And they were held in high esteem among the rulers; for from the illiterate is not to be expected the approval of a noble action, or mature consideration;

nay, on the contrary, there proceed from them various evils. The unwise have not the tact to acquire the desirable sufficient independence pleasing to the rulers. So an honored ruler, by keeping aloof from the unwise, can put himself in the way of acquiring the desired degree of excellence. His endeavors should not be directed towards any base or injurious ends, but he should strive by counteracting such tendencies to attain to a high position in the next world. Such a ruler gives good attention to the orders he issues and to other regulations (pertaining to the state); and thereby ensures a pleasant enjoyment of his dignity.

The (State-administering) chiefs should choose as their king a person of high rank and good repute. None but a man of worth should be elected king. For this purpose, a distinguished person related to the chiefs should be secured. Individual predilections should have no weight in the choice of a king. Further, if the person (fixed upon) is not of kingly descent, another one should be procured from a different place, as in the interests of justice the election (of a king) is indispensable.

To those wise men who choose to retire from the post conferred on them by the king, or who, in order that they may live in contentment, give up the business or service, which was entrusted to them, -- to those, that entertain such good notions of securing happiness, no benefit can accrue in life by this relinquishment (of their work). Because, if against their wishes they be again forcibly carried off by order of the State, and be forced to resume their work, they would find no enjoyment in it. Therefore they should stick to and perform faithfully whatever works appears to them to be of public or private benefit.

The learned kings of the State, with the view of ruling with a high degree of efficiency, should strive (for the fulfillment), by Divine Grace, of new and noble aspirations, such as: -- encouraging the learned, the illustrious, and the charitable, being grateful towards those who are loyal to and have affection for the State. Conferring of bounty on the suppliants and on those that are in solicitude owing to poverty, gratifying with a good and befitting remuneration annually, the learned men who may be in constant anxiety for having to labor for their food and livelihood, along with the giving of everyday donations, according to the needs of their circumstances. For the glorification of the (next) spiritual world to the conspicuous true believers who come into the (royal) presence, on those that arte misers greedy for amassing worldly pelf, on those that have no reverence for the soul. In addition, on those that abstain not from sins, nothing should be bestowed, so that they might not get facilities for taking to drink and of robbing the wise of their due.

Before putting a question in one's turn, one should catch the drift of the opponent's argument. Again, in a discussion, he that speaks much should not be checked, but his reasoning should be well listened to. Also, in a discussion, if there be a question, it should be satisfactorily answered. If there be many such questions they should be dealt with in various ways.

Every man that has a material body should regard his own marriage as a good work incumbent on him to perform. He should strive diligently at his avocation that he may live in happiness. He should take good care of the materials of power (i.e. good deeds for the next world) that his lifetime may pass in contentment. And he should promote the marriages of others.

If thou wish to be educated, give thy choice to the works of the foresighted (i.e. works pertaining to God). If thou wouldst avoid hard times, refrain from giving thy approval to works involving afflictions of various kinds.

Who are our instructors? The Dasturs learned in religion.

In what subjects have they to instruct us? In noble things (belonging to) three (places.)

Of all noble things and places, this world the next world and the transposing (i.e. the final imperishable embodiment).

Of what thing should we choose the good recompense? Of rightness.

How can we get instructions on this subject? From the Dastur of the religion says.

On our soul's parting from the body that will take us (to the spiritual world), and by what path, the good contriving quest (i.e. the guardian angel of the good conscience) by way (of Heaven), (Space the Universes around all things).

By what powers can we attain to the lodgment (within us) of good THOUGHTS? By the resolve of obedience of God, how can we acquire the resolve of such obedience?

By concentrated meditation through the acuteness of the intellect, I, for once, teach you two words of wisdom -- That you should do good deeds, and should refrain from doing deeds, which should not be done.

What deeds should we eschew and what deeds should we do? Evil THOUGHTS, evil words, and evil deeds we should eschew; and good THOUGHTS, good words, and good deeds we should adopt. Each of these maxims is good for you.

Chapter 3

AHRIMAN THE DESTROYER

Who is Ahriman? When did he come into existence?

Ahriman has been known by several names since 3000 BCE. Ahriman is also associated through other beings. Ahriman was created to bring fear.

It is said that Ahriman comes around every one thousand years to destroy or to take over Terra, and bring darkness to Terra for an unknown length of time. This has been interpreted many ways through the ages.

I can say this, since we entered into the twenty-first century, (and it is now 2004), that there is no being of evil destroying the earth and bringing darkness among the people. Also Ahriman has not made his presence known in the last two thousand years, neither have any demons or gods.

So, who and what is Ahriman? Ahriman is a manifestation of thought. Ahriman (negativity) is created by thoughts from all beings (by the people of Terra). People go about fearing a being of evil, and a being of good, which would come to Earth and create a battle between light and dark.

People do not realize the forces of energy and the magnitude of their own thoughts, effect what is being created. As everyone goes about fearing evil -- and the beings, that they (the people) are creating this evil (negativity) and the beings represent all of this fear.

What follows on these next few pages, are some ideas of what these beings look like based upon, what people are creating with their thoughts about those negative beings.

The pictures of negative beings are the same, generation after generation. Age after age, time and time again it never changes.

The stories that follow through the years are told, time and time again, about beings of good and dark coming to Earth, to battle among all beings.

These are some of the names that are associated with The End of Time, or in other words The End of an Age.

Kronos
Seth
Mephistopheles
Saturn
Ahriman
Lucifer

There are many other Names as well and many images.

A Journey into the Spiritual Quest of Who We Are – Book 3-
The Knowledge that was once forbidden by some of the Ancient Beings

At the end of every age, there have been some type of dark beings associated with bringing about famine, destruction, and other upheaval events. There are many stories of these beings that have been associated with all these changes. These changes are mainly normal changes of the Earth. But people need some type of being to blame for all these changes.

Kiazer had come to learn from his sojourn during his past thirty-seven years of delving deep into those stories. He has found how those stories became changed through the ages to make people fear these beings.

These are just a few drawing of what Kiazer found that deals with the typical ideas of these beings that people fear that are called devils

A Journey into the Spiritual Quest of Who We Are – Book 3-
The Knowledge that was once forbidden by some of the Ancient Beings

A Journey into the Spiritual Quest of Who We Are – Book 3-
The Knowledge that was once forbidden by some of the Ancient Beings

Ahriman, a being that is to come around, once every 1,000 years. So they say....

She is called Lilith. She is also seen around with Baal.

As Kiazer delves into those ancient stories, he comes across one of those typical stories, of how things were changed in the understanding of these beings.

When the Jews reached Canaan they changed from nomads to settled and agricultural people. Having no precedent of their own for agricultural pursuits or for the regulation of a settled life, it was inevitable that they should pick up many of the habits, customs, and attitudes of the natives of Canaan. The inhabitants of Canaan had a system of worship that paralleled that of Zarathustra, and worshipped Baal and the Baal's, with their female counterparts, chiefly Asteroth (Ishtar, Astarte). So did the Jews, but as time went on they converted the gods of the people among whom they had settled and with whom they had difficulties, into their own devils; just as the followers of Zarathustra had made of the gods of their Indian neighbors the devils of their own pantheon, and of the devils of their neighbors, their own gods. But it took some time to abolish the autochthonous deities found by the Jews in Palestine, especially since many of the Jews worshipped them. Thus we may read in Ezekiel that Jerusalem was a hotbed of pagans.

    Under Samuel, Saul, David, and Solomon, at the cost of incessant war and factional dispute, Israel was finally unified into a nation (Circa 1040, BCE). After the death of Solomon, who began to build the Temple at Jerusalem in 969, came the division of Israel into the two kingdoms of Judah and Israel. This was the period of the pre-exilic prophets, who gave statement to the fascinosum and tremendous aspects of the monotheistic deity Jehovah or Elohim, a word that originally meant gods in the plural. So in Amos, who flourished in the 8th century B.C.E?

    These beings of half human and animal, that people are socializing as evil / negative are totally wrong in that realization.

I talked about these beings in the first book a little. Some of these beings came into existence through the interaction of humans and animals. This was mainly due to the energy of Terra, changing and with Terra flipping on its axis, which had occurred during the time of 56,000 BCE, during the Second Age of Atlantis.

It was up to the guardians to help these beings to understand what happened to them and how they came to be in existence.

At the time of these beings deaths, it was also the task of these guardians to help separate these two beings souls, which were merged together as one.

Also at this same time, some of the Atlanteans scientists were playing around with genetic alterations. They created these same beings that nature once had a hand in creating. But these beings that these scientists were creating were more rebellious and destructive than their predecessors that were created by nature. These particular beings had gone into the world without the knowledge of why they were created. Moreover, they created havoc among the civilizations. This is where the people created those stories about these beings, which were of half human and animal.

These stories that were created were of negativity and evil. Mainly, because these beings left Atlantis and went to other continents. The inhabitants of those other continents knew nothing about these beings. These inhabitants were witnessing this destructiveness and chaotic events from these beings. And those stories are still told today without the understanding about these beings and how they came to be.

These beings are not evil by any means. Yes, they are different due to the type of energy that the Earth was entering at that time.

I urge all to learn and understand the truth about all these beings that existed during the old ancient ages of Terra.

This is the only way all will truly understand about the life that once existed, and the life that will become part of Terra again. It will also help you to understand the energy of the evolution process of life.

One thing for sure, you will not learn the truth of the ancient ages through your religions. They know about all of this, but they are the ones that are creating this fear towards these beings. So, the only way that is left for you to learn the truth is to go out and research it on your own.

There are many stories that are told about these ancient beings that existed eons ago, and they are not all true. The early stories are of negative, but if you keep on digging deeper into these stories, you will see that these stories will change from negative towards the positive. Then you will see for yourself on how these stories came to be changed. They were to create fear towards these other beings.

It is up to us the guardians to teach everyone the truth on how these stories of the old ancient ages were twisted and turned inside out. They were to bring about fear and confusion about all these beings that are in existence. Just because these beings are different, does not make them evil / negative at all.

    The task of these guardians was to untwist and teach the truth about the existence of life, of whom you all are (the human race), and to help you to understand about these other beings, which are among you today.

    Remember, all beings have a role to fulfill that exists. If it to be, within this plane that we exists on or if it is below or above us. This also goes for the beings that are moving from spirit to the first dimension and first to second dimension. Then the second to the third dimension and as the people of Earth are moving from the third to the fourth and fifth dimensions. You also have those beings going from the fourth and fifth dimensions, and moving to the sixth dimension, and so on.

    These beings are not what you and the religions are making them out to be. Yes, these types of beings do exist, like many other beings that you are not aware of at this time.

    The only dark and upheaval times that we are all witnessing on Terra are our own thoughts, which are being brought about by the religions and the governments of this world.

Chapter 4

The Ancient of Beings

Who are these ancient of beings?

These ancient of beings existed eon's ago, (100,000 plus years ago). Several of them are still among you today, while the other ancient beings had moved on to other dimensions. They also wait for you, too, to move foreword to the dimensions where they, the ancient of beings await, so they can teach you what they know of what is to come to you in the shifting, into the coming dimensions that await all of you.

Some of these ancient of beings, which are still among you, are from Atlantis, Lemuria, Mu and many other ancient races. Not all of these beings are of human form. You also have those beings that are mammals, such as your whales and dolphins. There are also races of beings that are of off worlds, like the Yeti (i.e. Bigfoot), the reptilian races, the lizards, and the Greys and many others.

On the next few pages we give you examples of these beings.

These beings are also of the higher realms of existence. They have been on other planes of existence, which was prior to your past existence, in the second and third dimensions. We are now entering the fourth and fifth dimensions of existence.

Who are these Avatars - Vishnu's, the ancient of beings? They were also known during the ancient times by being called (Prophets, Messiahs, gods, i.e.).

These beings may appear to be those that you would associate as being Angels, Avatars, Vishnu's, and other godlike beings. But, you should always keep in mind, they are not gods, just like the devils/demons, and they too are not what you make them to be.

They are known as beings that have godlike feats and powers, they are immortals, some of them are of human origin, others are humanoid in appearance, but not human. All of these beings are both positive and negative energies.

A Journey into the Spiritual Quest of Who We Are – Book 3-
The Knowledge that was once forbidden by some of the Ancient Beings

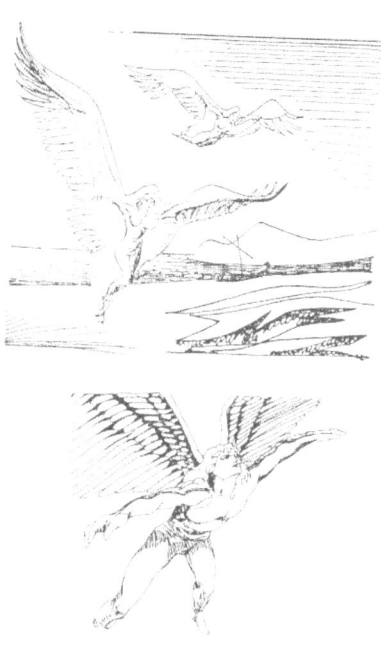

Male and Female, winged beings, called Zephyrs

The Human / Humanoid

A Journey into the Spiritual Quest of Who We Are – Book 3-
The Knowledge that was once forbidden by some of the Ancient Beings

Lemurian's

A Journey into the Spiritual Quest of Who We Are – Book 3-
The Knowledge that was once forbidden by some of the Ancient Beings

Half-breeds of Human / Humanoid

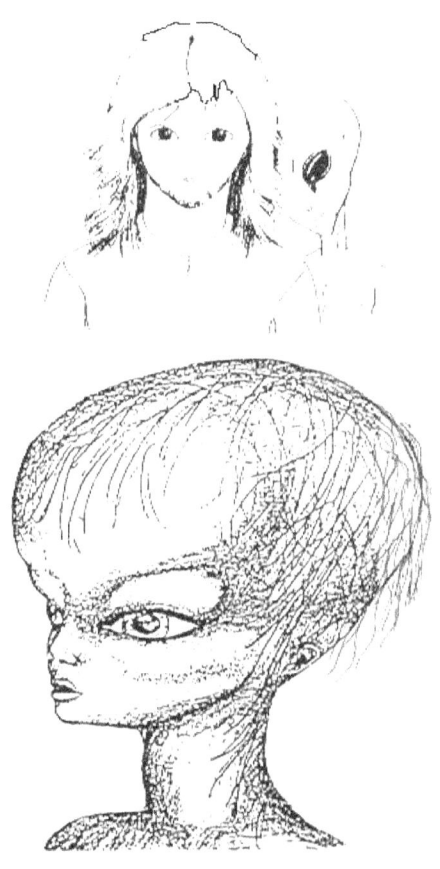

A Journey into the Spiritual Quest of Who We Are – Book 3-
The Knowledge that was once forbidden by some of the Ancient Beings

The various types of Grey's

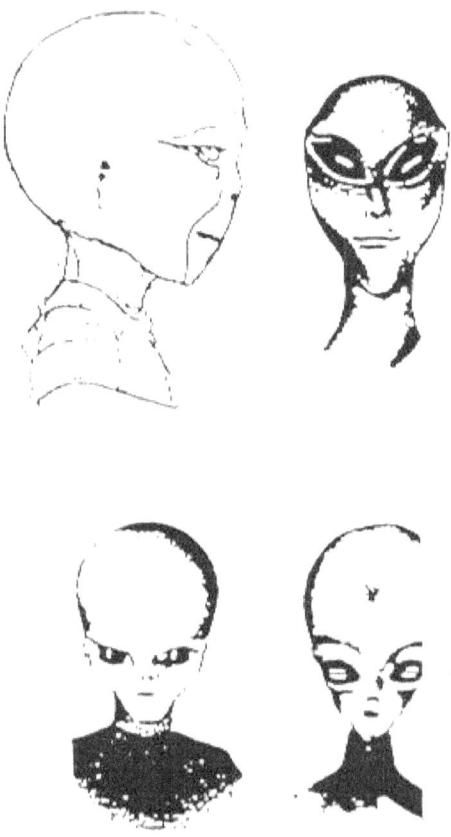

A Journey into the Spiritual Quest of Who We Are – Book 3-
The Knowledge that was once forbidden by some of the Ancient Beings

Half-breeds of Human and Animal

A Journey into the Spiritual Quest of Who We Are – Book 3-
The Knowledge that was once forbidden by some of the Ancient Beings

Top picture is a breed of Humanoid / Reptilian
Bottom is a breed of Humanoid / Serpent

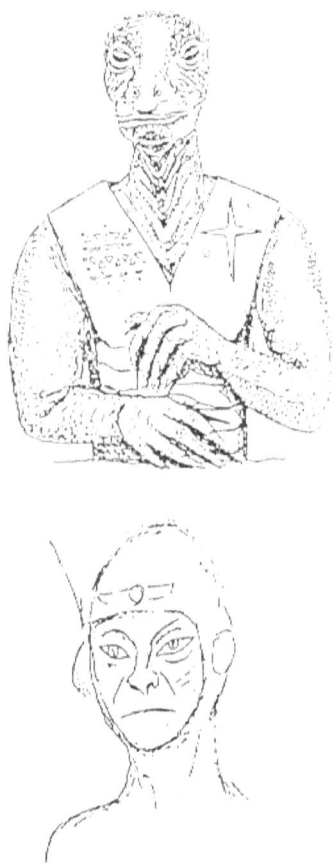

Eunuch - A being that is of both sex genders, you heard about these beings in the early stories of the Bibles.

Our Whales and Dolphins

Avatar

All of these beings once existed together several ages ago. And yes, these beings are still among us today, but they are not seen everyday in this day in age. This is due to one key factor, and that is that there is one race that fears all of these beings. This race also fears them.

This is one type of being that is known as the human race.

These Avatars existed secretly, no one really knows who they are. Except in the stories of the battles of light and dark that we read in mythology. Even those stories of myths are limited on talking about the Avatars, because the Avatars live their life in secrecy so they wont be noticed. But you might come across a couple stories of these Avatars if you dig deep enough into the ancient mythology stories.

I mentioned one of these stories about the Avatars in Book 2 in the second chapter.

Eons ago these ancient of beings had appeared at times, when civilizations were experiencing major upheavals and changes along with wars of dark times. They were known as Avatars, and they are of many races of human and humanoid types, such as elves, dwarves, changelings, and reptilian beings, along with many humans with godlike powers and many countless other beings, which will come to aid those races, that are on the planet. The Avatars are also bound by this positive and negative energy. So you will have stories of these beings creating chaotic events and these beings of light and dark challenging one another.

As I mentioned previously, most of these wars that these Avatars take part in are between themselves, which are fought in secrecy. Nevertheless, someone might come across, witnessing those battles, and they go about writing about them.

As we read those stories, and myths, about them from ages ago, most people look at these stories as myths, fairy tales, and as fantasy. But these stories are true. Just because these beings are not seen in our world of today does not mean they were not real, eons ago.

These beings existed, and people wrote about them in hoping that these beings would not be forgotten through the ages of the human civilization to come.

These stories are about these beings that came to the aid of the humans in their time of need. These beings were also the caretakers of balancing the positive and negative energies of Terra.

The aspects of these stories, that religions and most of the society of today, go about labeling these myths, as being of fairytales and saying that it is not true. Without realizing it, they are also labeling their stories of their bible as not being true as well, as a fairytale.

Within these stories of this so-called Bible, are of these beings, of pre-ancient civilizations. The Bible goes about telling of events that were passed down through the ages of the human race, about these off world human / humanoid beings. Moreover, if there was something they do not want to accept, then they go about hiding that information of knowledge, or they will just leave that part of it out of the story. Or they will go about turning those stories inside out.

So, the Bible is also telling about stories of myths, of a long time ago. However, the Bible is more of the current times, and people do not want to think that there were any other civilizations other than the current one.

These stories, of those ancient civilizations, of eons ago that we are learning about did in fact exist, and they are not fantasy.

Well, the civilization of today is all in for a big surprise. These stories of these myths of these ancient pre-civilizations and the beings are all true.

The religions and society go about labeling these myths of the pre-ancient civilizations, which existed prior to 12,000 and as far back as 100,000 years ago, as only being fantasy. Then they need to label those stories of their Bible as being as such. Since the entire Bible is the same, a compiled collection of modern stories of the same type of beings. It talks about pre-ancient stories, that people call stories of myths.

Once you start looking at all these stories of mythology, of the ancient times, that date before 12,000 years ago and prior, you will have a better understanding of those cultures and of what life is all about and the knowledge that these ancient beings possessed.

Chapter 5

Watchers

There is another group of beings that are always around, and have been since the starting of any civilizations in the universes. And these beings are on the so-called sideline. These beings are in the shadow so to speak, of all the events, and at times these beings will interact with the civilizations. These are the Watchers and they record all events that are transpiring, between the conflicts with other beings in the universes that are of the Earth and from other worlds that exist among the universes.

Who are the Watchers?

They are of the pre-Ancient civilizations. Known by Atlantis, Lemuria, Mu and many others of the pre-ancient times. The only ancient records that have been found were in the 1980's. They are those of the ancient Sumerians, of ancient Persia - also of Babylon and a few other pre-ancient cultures. These Watchers are also called NeTeR, which also means, Guardians. They have also been known as the Anunnaki's and as the Nefilem.

These Guardians are known to obtain the knowledge of life of the universes. These Watchers / Guardians have more knowledge about all aspects of life, the Earth, and about the stars, during their time, which dates over 50,000 years ago. Compared to what the people of Terra know and understand today, about life, and the universes around us.

It has been written during the ancient of days, about some of these beings of pre-ancient civilizations, which came down from heaven, (the stars).

One has to understand the terminology of the ancient times, and not what has been twisted and passed down by current times of terminology. These beings came down from heaven. Heaven actually means, from the stars. The only way that these Watchers, that are known as the Anunnaki / Nefilem, would have been able to obtain the knowledge of life of the universes is only by traveling the vastness of the universes. And the only way that this could be accomplished is by the use of starships.

There are also writings from the ancient of days of these crafts. And again we find the terminology not understood. We hear those stories, about the strange objects in the sky, such as:

They Followed the Bright Star -
The Wheel within A Wheel -
The Burning Shields -
Fiery Chariots -
They or He came out of a Cloud -

There are many other descriptions out there similar to these above.

All of these are descriptions of how these starships appeared to the humans during the ancient times. These are the ships of these beings that are from the stars.

What are the reasons for these beings, that are called the "Anunnaki / Nefilem - Watchers / NeTeR / Guardian," purpose for coming to Terra?

There are several reasons.

They are watching and recording the events that are taking place. Which are between the beings that are from other worlds and the actions of the people of Terra, with these beings?

Such as seeing how the people, of Terra are reacting to these so-called stories that were created eons ago, about the battles of good and evil that were created by these beings, of the so-called gods, that wanted to control this star system and create fear among the people, about these Anunnaki / Nefilem, and the Watcher / NeTeR / Guardians.

Your previous cultures wrote about and started religious belief systems, that were based on what these gods were telling people of Terra some 25,000 years ago - of what will happen in the future, and how they need to live their life. These watchers are also watching and seeing what the people of Terra are going to create for themselves in the coming of the New Age.

The people continue to live in fear of these so-called gods and devils and too continue to let these beings control their life from afar. They do so without even seeing these beings for the past two thousand years, and without knowing whom these beings are, which they fear so much.

Will the people continue to believe in these stories of the past? Will they live the same life as they have the past 25,000 thousand years? Will they take steps backwards in the evolution, to take part in another Dark Age, just to start over again?

Or will the people make a quantum leap foreword and let the old ways of life, which are of the third dimension, go by the wayside, so the people could make that quantum leap into fourth/fifth dimension of existence, which is a deeper understanding of spirituality of evolution? Which is becoming the being that you really are.

On the other hand, we might have Terra ripping apart to bring forth two planets. One world, will be back in the Dark Age, while the second world will be jumping forward into their quantum leap of spirituality, along with peace, light, and harmony.

These Watchers are also known to interact with the inhabitants from time to time, as you have read in the previous chapters and in the other two books.

These NeTeR went about teaching the habitants of this planet about the knowledge of life and of who you are, in the scheme of things. The NeTeR started the reawakening processes, about life, which laid dormant in all beings. The NeTeR knew by teaching the humans about life, that these beings that are playing gods, were in control of these star systems, and they do not like the idea of this knowledge of life, that was being taught to other races. Therefore, these gods made up stories to get the inhabitants in fear of these true beings of light, (NeTeR - Watchers and the Anunnaki – Nefilem), they were taught these beings were of evil.

Here is an interesting theory that I came across back around June of 1996. It deals with the songs of whales and the clicks and whistles of the dolphins. It is said that the whales and dolphins are the oldest mammals alive on the planet and that they are the remaining guardians of Terra. The songs that the whales sing fit right into what I mean about the knowledge of life.

Here is part of the research that Richard Butler is working on.

Dolphins of Heaven

It should also be noted that on the rare occasions that abductees hear verbal sounds from the Greys Beings it is described as high-pitched, sometimes chattering or staccato clicks or beeps. These are all similar to the air vocalizations of dolphins. The Greys are reportedly engaged in human / grey hybrid experiments. This is to combine the genetic material of both species into a hybrid species.

Is this possible? The Japanese and several other countries are working even now on interspecies hybridization's. If I am correct that the Greys are of dolphin decent, and then the possibility of successful hybridization becomes much greater. Some believe that on Terra, man shared a common genetic ancestor with the dolphin. Up to a certain point in development human and dolphin fetuses are nearly identical. In the not too distant future it will be possible to produce a hybrid human / dolphin species. It is Richard Butler contention that the Greys have already beaten us to it.

Finally I would like to point out that dolphins have been associated with the "gods" AKA the aliens, from earliest recorded times. Certain mythologies hold that some of the gods came from a world of water. It is now through by most that these beings genetically altered the existing pre humans on Earth.

(I showed this as well in my second book, why were they called gods.)

It is certain that the Greys would have had a hand in this. One of the greatest of ancient worship sites is the temple of Delphi. This was originally the temple of the sea goddess. The word Delphos means both dolphin and womb. Richard Butler believes it is time we stopped calling them Greys and use the proper name our ancestors called them. They knew of the gods who came from the water world in the heavens long ago. They called them Delphim. I hope that you have found this enlightening and thought provoking. For those out there who consider humans the only intelligent species on the planet, as Richard Butler demonstrate the power of the cetacean brain. The bible contains a little over a million and a half bits of information. The song sung by humpbacked whales contains over fifteen million. Each year it changes just slightly and every whale on the planet knows what those changes are. Now ask yourself this. Could you remember the bible word for word? Could you remember fifteen of them? Think about it. If our bible contains our basic history, social and religious philosophies, what does something fifteen times larger contain?

It is Richard Butler's deepest hope that this article will allow you to open new perceptions on the events now taking place on this planet to see both the Greys and yourselves in a new way. I think in time we will come to find that what is down here, is exactly what is out there. That there are humans, dolphins and other beings cooperating out there. Perhaps we should stop and ponder our roles as the caretakers of this planet. Man has hunted our own cetacean population to the very edge of extinction. It is something that we all must take shame in.

Recently efforts have been made by the civilized nations to preserve the great whales and dolphins. Can we live peacefully on this planet with another intelligent species? I truly hope so. I would hate for another more advanced species to treat us as well as we have treated the whales.

Many hope for contact with these beings. If we cannot get along with an indigenous intelligent species, how can we expect to get along with one of extraterrestrial origins? A people are judged by their actions. If we demonstrate our goodwill towards our fellow inhabitants of this world, perhaps those not of this world will be sent a message, that we are civilized after all.

What knowledge do these whales posses? One can only imagine the purpose of these whales and the songs that they sing. Man has always thought that they were the guardians of Terra.

How can something as primitive as man, be the guardian of Terra when all we care about is conquering and destroying all life, including our human species, along with the planet?

The only way that the human race will become the guardians of Terra is when they put an end to the governments and religions of the world, and recognize all life and live in peace with all. That goes for all life, human and animal.

Until that time comes, for the time being, these whales are the guardians, the caretakers of Terra. The songs that they sing balance Terra's energy, from all the destruction that man is doing to Terra.

At the same time, the whale's songs renounce a frequency, that which brings the human energy (frequency), to a higher state of consciousness. Which will bring the human race to awaken the knowledge of life, which lies dormant in all life.

The time of these whales as being the guardians of Terra will be ending soon.

They are imparting their knowledge about life to us. Are we ready to become that spiritual being, that we are, and finally become the guardians of this planet? This means making peace between all human beings, and ending this 3,000-year-old war, which was to see who could control and destroy one another.

We are all humans on this planet.

We are all one race, which is known as the human race. It does not matter what country you are from because we are all of one, which is the human race. If the human race ever wants to become the guardians of Terra, then all of you must first realize who you are. Then and only then, you will become who you are.

The main purpose of these Guardians is to help bring the human race to the understanding of who they are. The knowledge of life is for all to know, regardless of how some beings wanted to control and keep this knowledge as secret as possible.

At the end of every age/cycle, the NeTeR are found to be more present then at normal times, which is due to the changes that the human race and the star system go through, because what happens on Terra also effects everything outwards in a ripple effect as the same happens on other planets within all the universes.

Chapter 6

THE KNOWLEDGE

Through the ages of the human race there have been stories about the humans going about obtaining the knowledge of the gods, (The Ancient of Beings) beings which came from the stars.

Some of these beings from the stars did not take a liking to the other star beings. These other beings were trying to teach the other beings that were trying to obtain the knowledge that these star beings procured.

The common stories that are told age after age are of Adam and Eve, also known as the human race. There are also countless other stories as well, that are similar in story to one of them, which is The Tower of Babel of Babylon.

Everyone knows about the religious aspects of the story of Adam and Eve. That story deals with the negative and the fear of knowledge, along with two beings that represent good and evil, (positive and negative). Everything in the story of Adam and Eve, (the human race) is symbolical in nature and in life.

Well, here are the true aspects of that story.

There is no doubt that there were other beings that took part in persuading the early Adam and Eve to learn the Universal Knowledge of their life, along with the beings that did not want Adam and Eve to learn the knowledge of life.

Everyone knows about the serpent beings that were persuading Adam and Eve to eat of the fruit of the forbidden tree.

In actuality the serpent beings were not serpent. They were the beings of light, helping the human race, to break away from those beings that people called god, who was keeping them from learning of the knowledge of life.

In addition, the fruit was not actual fruit. It was the knowledge of life and of who they are.

Some beings were teaching Adam and Eve about the knowledge of life and who they are, the other being (that was called god) did not like the idea, and told Adam and Eve that those beings are of evil and they need to stay away from them and not to learn of the knowledge that those beings are teaching.

You would think that this so called (god) would want the human race to know the knowledge of life and of who they are. You would think that a benevolent being, (that is taking the role of i.e. god), would encourage the knowledge about life and of other worlds around other stars which hold life, but the opposite occurred. This being did not want the human beings to grow in knowledge and in spirituality. This being wants to create fear towards these other beings in anyway possible, including turning the story inside out, just to make the people fear those other beings that exist. Just so this being called god, could rule by fear, over these people and this planet/star system.

This so-called god tried to control Adam and Eve in thinking that those beings that were teaching this knowledge were evil.

In fact, this so-called god was deceiving them all, (the human race) on thinking this way.

We all know what happened then. The human race secretly met with these benevolent beings that were teaching them about the knowledge of life and about who they are in the scheme of life.

So, this so-called god learned of what Adam and Eve had gone and done. So this so-called god had punished them for disobeying their go, for going out and learning of this knowledge that they were told not to learn.

Now if this were a god of righteous and of truth, knowledge, and wisdom, then why would some of these beings go about keep all this knowledge from all the beings that wish to know of it?

Why should we accept this being as god, if all he does is punish all the beings (humans) for learning?

In fact, this so-called god is the deceiver of life. This so-called god should be the on that we should be avoiding, and not the others that we are being told to stay away from.

Now, for the aspects on the story of The Tower of Babel of Babylon, the humans attempt to rise up a Shem (Shem and the term shamain (heaven), stem from the root word shamah, meaning, that which is high ward).

The biblical tale of the Tower of Babel deals with events that followed the repopulating of Terra after the Deluge.
"Let us build us a city,
And a tower whose top shall reach the heaven;
And let us make us a Shem,
Lest we be scattered upon the face of the Terra,"
But this human scheme was not to God's liking. And the lord came down, to see the city and the Tower, which the Children of Adam, (the human race) had erected.
And he said: "Behold,
All are as one people with one language,
And this just the beginning of their understandings;
Now, anything, which they shall scheme to do
Shall no longer be impossible for them."
Moreover, the lord said to some of his colleagues...
"Come, let us go down,
And there confound their language so that they may
Not understand each other's speech,"
And the lord scattered them from there
Upon the face of the whole earth,
And they ceased to build the City.
Therefore was its name called Babel?
For there did the lord mingle the Earth's tongue."

This was done so the people would not understand one another's language. But in time we were able to learn each other's languages. This so-called god tried to prevent people from being one with each other. Nevertheless, this language barrier did not last long.

One thing remains for us today, which is to accomplish becoming one with each other, and putting aside our differences. That way what this so-called god did not want us to accomplish, did not work. It is taking us a while, but we will get there.

When you look at the word shem use "sky borne vehicle" rather than, "name" for the word shem, which is the term used in the original Hebrew text of the Bible. The story would then deal with the concern of humankind that, as the people spread upon Terra, they would lose contact with one another. Therefore, they decided to build a "sky borne vehicle" and to erect a launch tower for such vehicles. Like they are so called gods that they fly around.

Look at the Airships we have today.

In the story the "Epic of Creation" relates that the first "Gateway of the gods" was constructed in Babylon by the gods themselves. These gods were also known as the Anunnaki.

Which also ordered:
The construction of the Gateway of the gods....

Some time prior to the human race building their tower, which was known as the Tower of Babel, which was also built in Babylon, we had the same event going on here, several thousand years later, that had taken place with Adam and Eve.

The gods did not like the human race evolving to where they, (these so called gods), were at in knowledge. So, these so called gods came down to earth and tried to put a stop to the entire human race, from learning about the knowledge of life.

We hear about these events happening through out all ages including today. We do not have the problem of these so called gods coming down and keeping us from learning the knowledge of what life is about. But we do have the problem of the governments and religions that are keeping us from learning of the knowledge about life.

However, we do have the help of these same star beings that started teaching us way before the time of Adam and Eve, about the knowledge of what life is all about.

So what does all this mean? Some of these beings that are from the stars are going about creating fear, and those same beings are within our governments and religions around this world and others.

This means that they are bringing into manifestation and creating this idea that the humans should fear their gods, when these beings are playing the roles of these gods to get the human race to live their life in fear.

The religions go about telling the people that they need to live their life a certain way, the way that God wants them to live. And if they do not live by those standards that the religions dictates to the people, then their God will bring about punishment or God will bring about the End Times to the people of Terra for going against their God.

The next few pages are about the Ark of the Covenant and the stories that the Ark was used as a weapon.

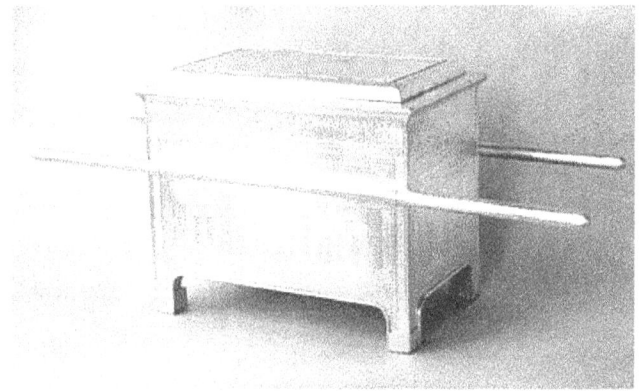

A model of the Ark

It is said that only the high priests were allowed near and to operate the Ark.

It is said that the Ark of the Covenant was actually a weapon and that only certain priests were allowed to carry the Ark.

When these priests carry this Ark into a city, and activate the energy of this Ark, the Ark starts to emit energy bolts from it, (like lightening) which come out of it and strike people, killing them. After this event was finished, the priest deactivated the Ark and left the city. All or most of the inhabitants were killed.

It is also said in these stories that this priest used this Ark to destroy and to level entire cities to rubble. Travelers at later time came upon these cities and found those inhabitants burned beyond recognition, and that the cities were in rubble.

Along with these stories, there are pictographs/drawings of this Ark being carried by priests and being taken into the cities and showing this Ark emitting lightening from it, and showing people being hit by this lightening and laying on the ground dead.

Some say this is the wrath of God killing people. Now tell me why this so-called god would want to kill the people of Terra?

The priests of the Ark would go about convincing those people of that age, that those people that the Ark had killed were wicked, and God killed them to set an example to the others, to hope to teach them not to disobey their God, or they will be punished or killed.

To this day, those religious people that live their life in fear of this so-called god go around killing people, time and time again.

This is a proven fact. That this so-called God, which had gone about killing people in the past for going against this gods so called belief structure, it is there in plain site.

This being that is called God, had gone about killing people, and destroying cities, and even going as far as annihilating all of civilizations on the entire world, at times.

For the question above, why is this god going about killing people and even destroying civilizations at times?

This is how I see it, and this is the truth!

So the human race would not learn about who they are, and about life. This was to keep the humans from becoming spiritually attuned and to keep them from their leap forward in spirituality.

This is why these Guardians are here on this planet and on many other planets as well. Which is to teach all life about their spiritual evolution of growth of life, despite what these so-called gods want.

Here is a story that all are familiar with. It's about the Ark of the Covenant of the gods.

This is an excellent story of the anger of the gods, with the human race that wanted to learn of the knowledge of life. Along with the NeTeR, that was teaching this knowledge to the human race.

This shows how far these so-called gods would go about protecting this knowledge. They will go about destroying all that want to learn of the truth of life. This also goes for all that teach about the truth of life. It is also known that these so-called gods will even go about destroying a planet. Just take a look at the Asteroid belt in your Solar System.

You can see an Ark of the Covenant in the city. The Ark is at left and in the middle, between the pillars. You can see some of the people removing those that are dead while others are weeping for those that this Ark had killed.

Below is a sketch of what the Tower of Babylon looked like.

When the so-called god came down and saw what the humans had erected, he did not take a liking to what they were doing. The god put an end to the construction...

You need to ask yourself the question, why would any being go about destroying the people or even the cities?

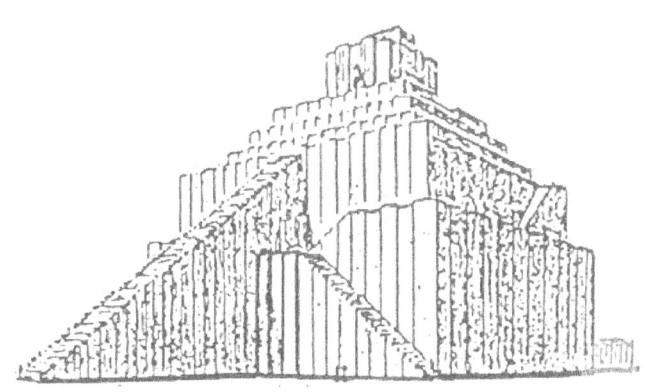

Chapter 7

Removing the Acknowledgment of Ancient Technology and Knowledge of Life

As you have read though out all three of these books, it is certain that there are beings in the universes that do not want other beings to evolve in their spiritual growth. There are other beings that promote this knowledge of spiritual growth, enlightenment, and who we all are.

You learned through these books about how some of these beings wanted to control all life on Earth and among the stars.

I have shown how all these stories of today came to be misinterpreted and how these stories became negative, from their original state.

I also brought to light that these beings that came from the stars, had the technology to travel the stars. They also obtain the knowledge from other beings of the universes, which they traveled to. Then they taught this knowledge to all other inhabitants of other star systems that they came upon. At the same time, these other star beings went against this teaching of this knowledge of life, which they had learned, through their journeys through the stars.

We know that the ancient Sumerians, back 7,000 years ago knew a lot more about the stars and planets than we know about the planets and stars in our day in age.

All this makes one wonder, how is all of this is possible?

Well, they had the technology of space travel. Which is the same technology that we are just learning about in the past 40 years and have very little understanding of it at this point.

So now one can ask, where is all this technology that these pre-ancient civilizations once had?

Or is this all someone's fantasy, about these pre ancient civilizations having this type of high space traveling technology? Do they have some other technology, as well to construct these large stone towers/pyramid cities and the knowledge about life?

Well, I can tell you that all of this is not a fantasy. It is all true. These pre-ancient civilizations did in fact have all this technology and the knowledge of what life is all about.

One can ask, if these ancient civilizations did have all this technology, then where is it?

On the other hand, did they take it all with them when they left Earth around 1000 B.C.E.?

My thoughts on this matter are my thoughts alone.

Some of this technology was left behind and it does exist, and the governments of Eria have recovered it. How did this government go about recovering this technology without the people realizing what our government is up to?

What is the one thing that draws everybody's attention away from everything else?

The answer is, WAR!

Then one can say, where do most of the wars that transpire take place? These wars take place on the continent of Tampaurban, around the locations of those ancient civilizations.

So, one might assume that these wars are a diversion to get people's attention drawn away from what is really going on, on the continent of Tampaurban. So as our attention is drawn to these wars, this so called secret government is taking this ancient technology out of that continent. And at a later time they will study it, and learn how it works, than they will develop this technology, and use it any way they chose.

This all makes you wonder. Look at the technology that our government/scientists have developed over the past 60 years, since the 1950s. One can only wonder where that technology came from. There is new technology that has been in the proto type for the past 20 years, which is just being made known to the people, now, in 2004.

So you can wonder again, what is our government really up to, and what type of technology are they developing now, based on what they are taking? Where will this new type of technology take us, in say the next 20-30 years?

Then one can ask another question.

What happens to these ancient cities after the government takes the technology that was left by these star beings?

Well, they might go about destroying the evidence that talks about this technology/knowledge, which may be part of a wall, which will show this technology?

Or, they might even go as far as destroying the whole entire city to rubble?

They might even bury the city, by moving, thousands and thousands of tons of sand.

I feel that our government in the U.S. will do just about anything to get the technology they want, and they will cover up where they are getting this technology from, that they are developing.

One can also wonder, what this technology that our government/scientists are developing, is going to be used for?

We know for sure, that these pre-ancient civilizations had this technology, and the knowledge about life, because their knowledge of the stars, dates back well over 12,000 years. We are just literally, beginning to learn about our star system since the 1700's. And we are still in the beginning stages, the kindergarten grade, of learning about space travel, and about ourselves..

These beings of these ancient civilizations were at a hundred times in their knowledge of the universes and of understanding who they were, and who we are today.

All this makes one think, what is life about? What is not being told to us? Why are the religions around the world trying so hard to hide this knowledge about who we are, and about life?

This knowledge of life is for all to know, no matter what.

Chapter 8

ESSENCE OF OUR EXISTENCE

What is this essence? This essence is the existence of all life. It binds all life together. Be it human, animal, plant, water, land, and the positive and negative energy of the universes. Our existence is all part of this essence of life. All essence is of positive and negative energy. This essence, energy of life, makes us what we are and how we interact with life? This essence molds the energy, which creates our lives from our very being and it guides us through our existence that brings about our journeys, which make up our destiny.

Through this essence of energy we our guided to experience events in our lives, be it of positive and or negative energy, (experiences). This energy of life shapes us into what we will become later. It's based on how we experience this energy of positive and negative, which binds all life together, in one form or another. How we experience this energy will determine the outcome of the experiences, along with how long we go through the experience. Which is also based on how we acknowledge the experiences that we witness, through our journeys in life.

There is one favorite saying about the aspects of negativity-but also true with the other energy, positive.

Once you start down the path of darkness, which is (fear, hate, and anger) forever consuming you. Moreover, it will become part of your destiny of who you will become.

Both paths of this essence of life are positive and negative energy. The path of the positive is that of mind at peace, love, tranquility, and harmony. And the path of negative is that of, hate, anger, confusion, and destruction.

The path of negative energy is subtler in making the person think that this path is the easiest to go through. But in fact it is the quickest. Mainly because it can make the person think what their experiencing is for the better, and that it is the easiest to comprehend. But in fact it is the harder of the two experiences.

These are the paths of the essence of life. We all end up going through them at one point in our life regardless if we want to or not. We cannot pick and choose which ones we want to avoid.

It is how we go about experiencing from interacting with the essence of life that will dominate one way or another. Nevertheless, we all have this free will to change our experience and our existence to one form or another.

REMOVING ALL VEILS

Wonder why all this fear about teaching this knowledge of life, which these so-called gods possess? Why do some of these beings that are playing these roles of gods, fear those beings that are teaching this knowledge?

If all beings understood about the knowledge of who each of us are, (meaning you, all beings of life), then these so-called beings that think they need to play the roles of gods and devils would fail. Their main proposes is to create fear and control over life, just to show other beings that are in control of life in the universes.

No one has the right to control another being that wants to learn all aspects of life. This also goes for these beings that are playing the roles of gods and devils. They think they need to control life with their fears.

Everyone has the right to ask questions about life, and they should receive the right answers, the truth, and not the lame excuses that they go about telling people.

If you think that this knowledge is of evil, then you are going down the wrong path. God wants you to go this way. You should not be asking those questions. We cannot talk about those things. People are told by their religions that they need to stay clear of anyone that is involved in the aspects of the supernatural or the spiritual/metaphysical part of life and the list goes on with out end.

The existence on Terra and any other planet or plane of existence is to learn and to grow in knowledge and in spirituality.

Nevertheless, it appears that some of these beings do not want that.

Why are the religions and the governments so desperate to keep this knowledge from the people at any cost, which includes lies and deception, just to control the people?

With all this in mind you will come across religions saying all this is impossible, this cannot be done. The only reason they say this is because, the religions teach that light/dark and positive/negative are two separate beings and not one being.

This is why religions were created, to bring about fear and confusion. This was to keep all beings from becoming the spiritual beings that you are.

I urge all to learn the truth of what the knowledge of life holds for all to experience. Along with the acknowledgment of what this essence of life is about. You will learn the true essence of your being of becoming these spiritual beings that all of you are.

In addition if you break away from these religions, you will start to see this truth. At that time you will start your reawakening of your knowledge of the essence of life, and of whom you are, along with what you are able to become and do, as the being that you are.

Now, what follows are the key factors for going about removing the veils that are keeping you from moving forward in life and becoming the spiritual being that all of you really are.

You have come this far in life. You have been here lifetime, after lifetime living the same way, which is being controlled on how to live your life.

You owe it to yourself to step up and remove these veils that keeps you from being who you are.

Now this is the time that all of you shall begin your reawakening. Start removing these veils that have been placed on you by these other beings that want to keep you from learning of who you are.

What Knowledge did these Benevolent Beings procure during their existence, then and now, about the existence of life?

The Ancient of Beings learned that life is energy, and that all beings and all aspects of life (humans (on or off the planet), animals, plants, and planets) are connected to each other including, all-positive and negative energies. We give our essence to create negative energies, and we can cease this energy from being created, which takes away the negative form.

By doing this we need to accept that we created all this, positive and negative energies and that we all are of one essence, energy.

In the Kabala, it teaches that the Armageddon, the battle of good and dark, will be fought in everybody, and in their soul.

The evil/negativity exist in all of us. If we deny this, we give evil power over us.

Once this is accepted, then you defeat it, and destroy the evil/negative energy.

This is the way you need to accept, this evil/negative energy, in order to become that spiritual being that you are to become!

I become one with everything,
I become one with you.
I become everything,
Therefore I become nothing.
Therefore you are nothing.
Without my anger, you have no substance.
Without my pride, you have no form.
Without my hate, you have no being.
Its time for you to leave.
You have no place here.
I'm apart of you now.

Once you come to terms with this understanding of the above, that (evil), negativity is part of you.

From this you bring life into the existence of this negativity energy. You had separated yourself from this negativity, without realizing that this is also part of you as well.

This is where religions keep you in the dark, on telling you that positive and negative are of two separate beings/entities. They are only separate entities, by the means of their teachings, only. This is what religions do not want you to understand and to learn.

You must understand fully of this concept, that you are the creator, of everything around you, along with the persons next to you, so on and so on, they too, are also the creators, of the things around them. Then we are all creators experiencing each other's creations.

After truly learning of this knowledge, then you can know who you are, and what we are capable of becoming.

After you have accepted and understood this knowledge of life, then you would truly know who you are, along with what life is about.

Which is that the future and the past, are all part of the now, and that we all are the giver and the taker, and that we all can be in many places at once, that we all are the masters of our own fate. We are the Creator and the Creation.

From all this brings the knowledge that you are the god that you are seeking outside of yourself. You are your own creator.

This understanding of this knowledge is not easy, and it does not come overnight. The knowledge of life comes with the experience of life.

Some people, those of the religions, say this knowledge is not for us to learn at this time. And the only time that we can learn this knowledge is when we pass away, from this existence. Well, why wait to learn the knowledge of life after you pass away?

Why put off until later, when you can do it now?

Now, learn the Knowledge of Life, and know, who you are!

As you learn this knowledge, you will be removing the veils of illusions of life.

Ever going forward

This is not the end!
This is not the beginning of the end!
This is the end of the beginning!

It does not end here. It ever goes on. Always going to the beyond the beyond. From one existence of life, to another life, so on, so on. Never ending with only one life or even with many lives. Life is like a ladder, each step is a life that you, we, all go through and experience.

Learn of who you are, this can be reawakened at this point in your life.

There is no god that will come to Terra and punish you for learning of the truth, as I had brought to your attention through out these books. For the past 3,000 years, there has not been any presence of these gods, making themselves known too the world, at this day in age.

Nevertheless, you are told through your religions that you must obey these so-called gods, or be punished.

So, why is there all this fear towards these so-called gods that you cannot see?

The wait is over, take this next step and learn, reawaken the knowledge within you.

This knowledge of life is there for all to know. And for all to become, that being that you are.

The thought,
Brings the experience,
Into existence.
Which starts a chain reaction.
As it brings forth knowledge,
Which reawakens who we are,
Bringing total awareness.
All veils are removed.

Look for the continuing series that continues with – A Journey Into The Spiritual Quest of Who We Are – Book 4 The Quantum Leap into Consciousness

A Journey into the Spiritual Quest of Who We Are – Book 3-
The Knowledge that was once forbidden by some of the Ancient Beings

www.ingramcontent.com/pod-product-compliance
Lightning Source LLC
Chambersburg PA
CBHW051450290426
44109CB00016B/1693